The Ancient Hebrew Language and Alphabet

Understanding the Ancient
Hebrew language of the
Bible based on Ancient
Hebrew Culture and
Thought

Jeff A. Benner

+

The Ancient Hebrew Language and Alphabet

About the cover: Photo taken at the University of Pennsylvania, Museum of Archeology and Anthropology by the author. The inscription reads "Sh'ma" meaning hear (see Duet 6.4) and is inscribed on a piece of broken pottery dated 586 to 450 BCE.

Cover and Illustrations by the author

"The Anicent Hebrew Language and Alphabet," by Jeff A. Benner. ISBN 1-58939-534-4.

Manufactured in the United States of America.

To my wife Denise, who has taught me more about Hebrew thought through her actions then all the books I have read.

Table of Contents

List of Illustrations

Introduction

This book is unique in that it will look at the Biblical Hebrew language of the Bible through the eyes of the Ancient Hebrews who wrote it. Modern readers often ignore the fact that the Bible is an Ancient text and must be read as an Ancient text. The definitions of Hebrew words, just like any other language, change and evolve over time. It is the goal of this work to bring out the Ancient Hebrew meanings of words to the student of the Bible as never before done.

The study of the Ancient Hebrew language and alphabet begins with an understanding of the Ancient Hebrew culture as both are intimately related. The original letters of the Hebrew alphabet was actually pictures, or pictographs, similar to Egyptian Hieroglyphs. Each picture represented an object whose definition is closely related to the agricultural lifestyle of the Ancient Hebrews. By studying the culture and lifestyle of the Ancient Hebrews we can better understand their language.

In a work such as this, there will undoubtedly be some misinterpretation of the Ancient Hebrew culture and pictographs. The study of any Ancient culture is like putting together a puzzle. We will never have all the pieces to the puzzle, but the pieces we do have, we piece together and attempt to fill in the gaps as efficiently as possible. Sometimes the gaps in the puzzle are small and easy to fill in based on the pieces around it. At other times these gaps are large and difficult to fill in. There is much work to be done in this area of language and word study and I hope that others, who have the same love for the Ancient Hebrew language and culture, will take on the challenge of continuing the research needed to piece together the puzzle.

One - The Hebrews

Who were the Hebrews?

The first person mentioned in the Bible as a "Hebrew" is Abraham[1].

> *"One who had escaped came and reported this to Abram the Hebrew"*. (Genesis 14.13)

Is Abraham the first Hebrew? The Hebrew word for "Hebrew" is עברי / eevriy[2] and comes from the root word עבר / avar which means, "to cross over". A Hebrew is "one who has crossed over". One of Abraham's ancestors was Eber[3] (עבר).

---

[1] Known as Abram before God changed his name.
[2] The letter ב (beyt) is pronounced as a "b" when at the beginning of a word, and usually a "v" within a word.
[3] Genesis 11.16

The name Eber also comes from the same root עבר / avar, making it possible that Eber was also a "Hebrew". The Bible is the story of God and his covenant relationship (Hebraicly understood as "crossing over" from death to life) with an ancestral line beginning with Adam through his descendants Noah, Abraham, Isaac, Jacob and Jacob's descendants, who became the "nation of Israel" also known as "the Hebrews". A Hebrew was one who had "crossed over" into a covenant relationship with God, beginning with Adam. Any references to the "Ancient Hebrews" in this book, is referring to the ancestral line from Adam to the Nation of Israel.

The Origin of the Hebrew Language and Alphabet

Prior to the incident of the Tower of Babel, which will be discussed later, only one language existed;

> "*And the whole earth was of one language, and of one speech.*" (Genesis 11.1)

From this we can conclude that God, Adam and Eve and their descendants spoke Hebrew.

The first use of the Hebrew language is recorded in Genesis 1.3 where God says, יהי אור (yehiy or), meaning, "light exist". In the creation account God gave Hebrew names to the sky (shamayim), land (erets), sun (shemesh), moon (yerey'ach), stars (kokhaviym) and man (adam). When God formed Adam he gave him this spoken language and communicated with him (Genesis 1.28). The man also used this same language to give names[4] to

---

[4] Genesis 2.19

4

all of the birds (oph), animals (behemah), beasts (hayah sadeh) and woman[5] (iyshah).

The first indication of writing is found in Genesis 4.15 where God puts a "mark" on Cain. The Hebrew word for "mark" is אות / owt and is also the Hebrew word for a "letter" indicating that it may have been a "letter" that God placed on him.

As will be demonstrated later, the Ancient Hebrew language (speech) and alphabet (script) are dependent upon each other, supporting a simultaneous appearance of the language and alphabet. Since God is the originator of the Hebrew language, he is also the originator of the alphabet.

Pre-flood writings have been discovered in the city of Kish[6] (fig. 1). Several of the letters in this tablet are identical to the original Hebrew letters[7] (See Appendix D).

Figure 1 Pre-flood pictograph found in the pre-flood city of Kish.

---

[5] Genesis 2.23
[6] Henry H. Halley, Halley's Bible Handbook (Grand Rapids, Mi: Zondervan, 24th) 44-5.
[7] Over time all alphabets evolve. Therefore, it is possible for the writing system of Noah's day to differ from the alephbet given to Adam.

Genesis chapter 5 gives a genealogical record from Adam to Noah where we find that all the names are Hebrew. We know that these names are Hebrew rather than another language because all of the names have meaning only in Hebrew and are related to their character as described in the Biblical text. For instance, the Hebrew name Adam means "man" and he was the first "man". Methuselah means "his death brings" and the flood came in the year that he died. Noah means "comfort" as he will bring comfort to his people[8].

Noah had three sons, Shem, Ham and Japheth. It is during their lives that God brought the great flood[9] because of man's wickedness. Only Noah and his family were spared. God commanded Noah and his descendants to:

"be fruitful and increase in number and fill the earth" (Genesis 9.1)

Noah's descendants remained in the area known as Mesopotamia[10]. Here man began to build the "Tower of Babel". In order to cause the descendants of Noah to scatter and fill the earth, God said, "let us go down, and there confound their language, that they may not understand one another's speech"[11].

After the incident of the Tower of Babel, which occurred around 4,000 BCE[12], we find three major languages, each

---

[8] See Genesis 5:29
[9] A literal flood that covered the whole earth. See The Genesis Flood by John C. Whitcomb and Henry M. Morris.
[10] A Greek word meaning "between (meso) rivers (potamia)", the land between the Tigris and Euphrates rivers.
[11] Genesis 11.7
[12] Merrill F. Unger, "Tower of Babel," Unger's Bible Dictionary, 1977 ed.: 115. (BCE - Before the Common Era, equivalent to BC)

very different and unrelated to each other[13]; Egyptian, Sumerian and Hebrew. The arrival of the Egyptian and Sumerian languages seems to have mysteriously appeared out of nowhere. It is interesting to note that while all three have a very similar pictographic[14] form of writing, the sounds for each of the letters are different, possibly indicating the method which God used to confuse the language of men.

As a result of the Tower of Babel man began to migrate in three different directions from Mesopotamia, just as God planned (fig. 2). The Shemites[15] were the descendants of Shem, traveling west speaking Hebrew. The Hamites traveled south into Africa and became the Egyptians speaking Egyptian. The Japhethites traveled north becoming the Sumerians[16], probably a sub-group of the Scythians[17], speaking Sumerian. In Genesis 10 we find the "table of nations", a record of the scattering of the descendants of the sons of Noah.

---

[13] J.I. Packer, Merril C. Tenney, William White, Jr., Nelson's Illustrated Encyclopedia of Bible Facts (Nashville: Thomas Nelson, 1995) 337; Unger, "Egypt," 288.

[14] A word of Greek origin meaning picture-writing where a picture represented a sound or combination of sounds. The Sumerian pictographs evolved into the cuneiform (wedge-shaped) writing familiar to most people.

[15] The Shemites (aslo called Semites) are the Hebrews. Later cultures, such as the Phonecians, Canaanites, Akkadians, Moabites, Amonites and Arameans sprouted out of the Hebrews and are also part of the Shemitic family.

[16] The land of the Sumerians was known as Sumer, which is Shinar in the Bible (Genesis 10.10) also known as Babylonia. It is believed that the Japhethites traveled north the Black and Caspian seas and are the ancestors of the Sumerians. See Unger, "Scythian," 987 and Madelene S. Miller and J. Lane Miller, "Sumer," Harper's Bible Dictionary, 1973 ed.: 710.

[17] Unger, "Scythian," 987.

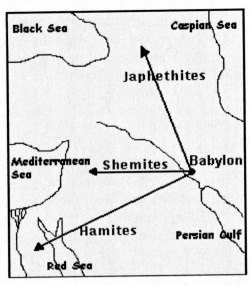

Figure 2   The scattering of the descendants of Noah's three sons.

It is not until we come to Noah's grand-children that we find names that are of a language other then Hebrew, such as Nimrod[18] (Genesis 11.8), Sabteca[19] (Genesis 10.7) and many others whose names have no meaning in Hebrew[20], correlating in time with the confounding of the language at the Tower of Babel.

It has long been a tradition within both Judaism and Christianity that Hebrew is the mother of all languages[21].

---

[18] See Strong's #5248
[19] See Strong's #5455
[20] The construction of Hebrew words, including names, follows a set of patterns. Words that do not follow these patterns are suspect of being of foreign origin.
[21] Will Smith, "Hebrew Language," <u>Smith's Bible Dictionary</u>, 1948 ed.: 238.

The evolution of the Hebrew alphabet

The original pictographic script (fig. 3) of the Ancient Hebrew alphabet[22] consisted of 22 letters, each representing an object such as water (top left corner) or a shepherd staff (second from right at bottom).

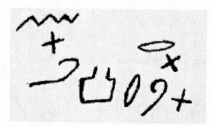

Figure 3 Ancient Shemitic/ Hebrew pictographic inscription on stone boulder c. 1500 BCE

After the Tower of Babel, the Ancient Hebrew alphabet began to evolve into a simpler script (fig. 4) similar to the original pictographic alphabet.

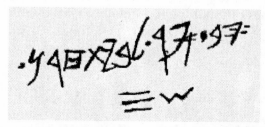

Figure 4 Ancient Hebrew inscription on potsherd c. 900 BCE

The Hebrews splintered into sub-groups such as the Phoenicians, Canaanites, Akkadians, Moabites (fig. 5), Ammonites (fig. 6), Arameans (fig. 8), and others, all

---

[22] Also known as "Shemitic", Semitic" "proto-siniatic", proto-canaanite" and "paleo-hebrew".

known as Shemites. Due to the close proximity and interaction of these Shemitic cultures, their alphabet script evolved similarly.

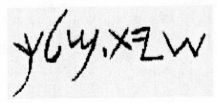

Figure 5 Moabite inscription on stone c. 900 BCE

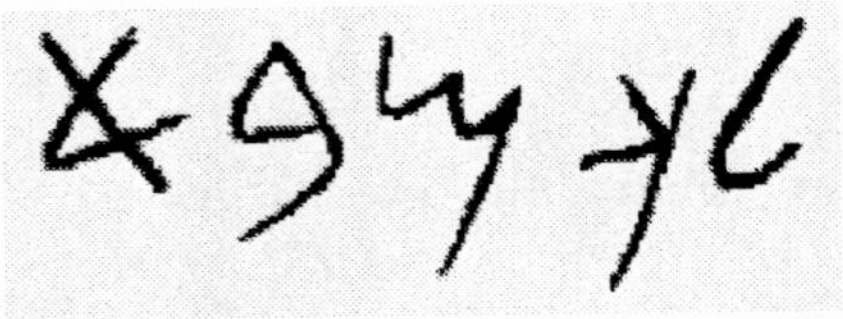

Figure 6 Ammonite inscription on stone   c. 900 BCE

At other times, alphabet scripts evolved very differently. The most unique is the Ugaritic, consisting of 30 letters where the original pictographic script evolved into a cuneiform[23] script[24] (fig. 7) sometimes called Hebrew cuneiform.

Figure 7 Ugarit cuneiform inscription on clay tablet c. 1400 BCE

---

[23] Cuneiform, meaning, "wedge-shape", is written with a stylus that is pressed into a clay tablet to form the letters.
[24] Because the Ugarit language is so similar to Hebrew, the Ugarit cuneiform is called Hebrew cuneiform.

Jeff A. Benner

The Aramean script (Aramaic), used extensively in the
Babylonian region, originated in the Hebrew script around
1000 BCE (fig. 8) and began to evolve independently of
other Shemitic groups. By 400 BCE it no longer
resembled the original pictographic script (fig. 9).

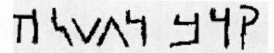

Figure 8 Aramaic inscription on stone incense altar c. 500 BCE

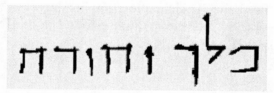

Figure 9 Aramaic inscription on stone plaque c. 20 CE.

When the Hebrew people were taken into Babylonian
captivity, they adopted the Aramaic script abandoning the
Ancient Hebrew script. From this point to the present, the
Hebrew language has been written in the Aramaic script
(fig. 10).

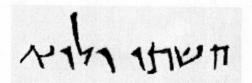

**Figure 10   Hebrew writings from the Dead Sea Scrolls c. 200
BCE**

11

The Modern Hebrew script has remained very similar to the Hebrew of the first century BCE (fig. 11).

בראשית ברא אלהים

Figure 11   Modern Hebrew script from the Hebrew Bible.

While the majority of the Hebrew texts of the first century BCE and into the first century CE were written in the Aramaic script, the Ancient Hebrew pictographic script was not lost and was still used on occasion. The coins of this era used the Ancient pictographic Hebrew script as well as some scrolls such as those found in the Dead Sea caves (fig. 12).

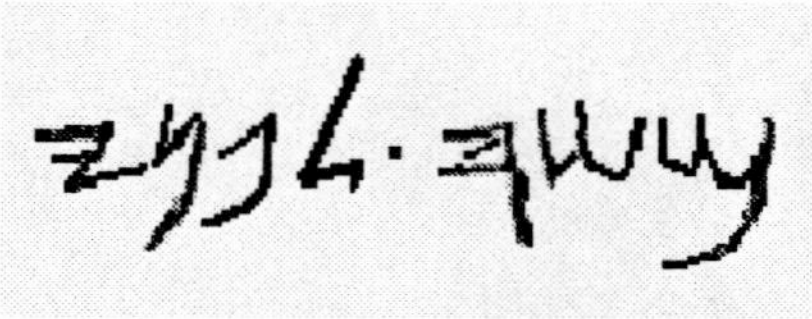

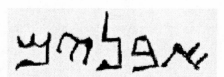

Figure 12   Pictographic Hebrew writings from the Dead Sea Scrolls c. 100 BCE

The Samaritans lived in the land of Samaria, a region of Israel, at the time of Israel's captivity; they were not taken into Babylon with Israel. As a result of their isolation they are the only culture to retain a script (fig. 13) similar to the Ancient Hebrew script and is still used to this day.

Figure 13 Samaritan scripts

Around 1000 BCE, the Greeks adopted the Ancient Hebrew script (fig. 14). This Ancient Greek alphabet began to evolve over the centuries to become the Greek script (fig. 15) used today. While all the Shemitic scripts shown above were usually written from right to left, they were written from left to right at times[25]. The directions of the letters reveal the direction of writing. For example, figure 14 was written from right to left. Note the direction of the "E" (first letter from the right) and the "K" (fifth letter from the right). Compare these with the same letters in figure 15, which is written from left to write. Note the "K" (first letter from the left) and the "E" (fourth letter from the left). Around 500 BCE the Greeks finalized a left to right form of writing while the Shemites finalized a right to left form of writing.

Figure 14 Greek inscription found on bowl c. 800 BCE

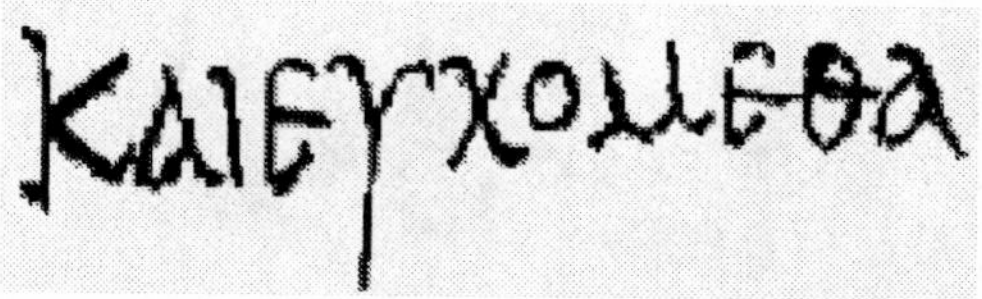

Figure 15 Greek writing on New Testament papyrus c. 200 CE

---

[25] Ancient inscriptions were often written on stone using a hammer and chisel. Since the hammer was held in the right hand and the chisel in the left hand, a right to left writing was natural. When ink began to be used, it was preferable to right from left to right so that the hand would not smear the ink.

To the south of the Shemitic peoples, the Egyptians were writing with an alphabet almost identical to the Ancient Hebrew script. In addition to the alphabet, the Egyptians used a complex system of pictographs called hieroglyphs (fig. 16) where each pictograph represented one, two or three syllables.

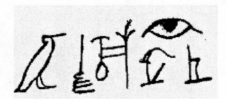

Figure 16   Egyptian Hieroglyphs from the Book of the Dead c. 1350 BCE

To the east of the Shemites were the Sumerians whose system of writing was very similar to the Egyptian with several hundred pictographs (fig. 17). Over time, these pictographs evolved into a cuneiform script (fig. 18) similar to the Ugaritic.

Figure 17   Sumerian Pictograph on clay tablet c. 3000 BCE

Figure 18 Sumerian Cuneiform on clay tablet c. 2500 BCE

Due to the common origin of all the scripts above, similarities of the script of different cultures can be observed. One example is the letter "lamed" that can be seen in several of the inscriptions above, as well as noting its similarity to our "L".

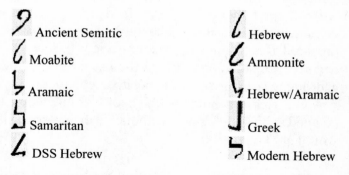

Since the Egyptian, Sumerian, Greek, Aramaic, Arabic, Hebrew and other Shemitic cultures have their origins in the Ancient Hebrew script, tracing their history and evolution is beneficial to reconstructing the original Ancient Hebrew script. Appendix "C" includes a set of two charts for each of the 22 Hebrew letters. One chart includes all the known scripts of 14 languages. The other is a flowchart showing the evolution of the letter through the centuries

Why study the Ancient Hebrew language and culture?

The Hebrew people, whose culture and lifestyle were very different than our own, wrote the Bible between 1,500 and 500 BCE.

When we read the Bible as a 21st Century American, our culture and lifestyle often influence our interpretation of the words and phrases of the Bible. A word such as "rain" has the meaning; "the coming down of water from the clouds in the sky", but the interpretation of the word rain will be influenced by the context of the culture. This is true even in our own culture where the word "rain" can be interpreted differently. If the local weather station forecasts a "rain" shower for tomorrow, different people will interpret the word "rain" in different ways, with a circumstantial biasness. The bride and groom who are prepared for an outdoor wedding view this news with a negative connotation, while to the farmer in the middle of a drought season, it has a positive connotation. To the Ancient Hebrew nomads the word "rain" was usually equated with "life" since without it, their very existence would not be possible.

Another example of the importance of understanding the cultural setting can be seen in the word "dinner". To my grandparents and their generation, "dinner" was the main meal of the day eaten at noon and a light "supper" was eaten in the evening. Where as today, dinner is the main meal eaten in the evening. There are countless examples in our own English language of how word meanings change over time according to the culture.

Many times our cultural influence will give a different definition to words that was not intended by the Biblical authors. For example the Bible speaks of keeping and breaking the commands of God. The words "keep" and "break" are usually interpreted as "obedience" and "disobedience". But this is not the Ancient Hebraic meaning of these words.

The Hebrew word for word "keep" is שמר / shamar) which literally means "to guard, protect, and cherish" while the Hebrew word for "break" is פרר / parar and literally means "to trample underfoot". The Ancient Hebrew understanding of these words is not about mechanical obedience and disobedience of his commands, but ones attitude towards them. Will you cherish his commands or throw them on the ground and walk on them?

A people's language is very related to their culture, without an understanding of the Hebrew culture we cannot fully understand their language. To cross this cultural bridge, we need to understand the Ancient Hebrew culture, lifestyle and language.

How do we study the Ancient Hebrew language and culture?

Archeologists who uncover Ancient artifacts study the Ancient cultures. Anthropologists interpret these artifacts to determine the Ancient culture's way of life. Throughout the world there remains primitive cultures whose lifestyles have remained the same for thousands of years, providing us with a close up view of how these Ancient cultures lived. One of these groups is the desert nomad of the Middle East who still live much the way Abraham did over 3,000 years ago. Linguists and etymologists study the ancient languages, opening the door to their manner of speech and alphabets. Many Ancient cultures have left ancient texts recording their thoughts and lifestyle. The most notable text of the Ancient Hebrews is of course the Bible.

When we combine and study the material provided by these fields of study, we open the door to the culture and lifestyle of Ancient cultures. By studying these resources we can better understand their words, which they have recorded in the Bible. The purpose of this book is to teach the relationship between the Hebrew language and the Hebrew culture, which will give us a deeper, more accurate, understanding of Biblical words.

Two - Hebrew Thought

In the world, past and present, there are two major types of cultures; East (Hebrew), such as today's oriental cultures of the Far East, and West (Greek), such as Europe and America. Both of these cultures view their surroundings, lives, and purpose in ways that would seem foreign to the other. The Ancient Hebrews were Eastern thinkers, more closely related to today's Orientals than Americans or even Modern day Hebrews in Israel, which has adopted a western culture.

What happened to this Ancient Hebrew thought and culture? Around 800 BCE, the Greek culture arose in the north. This new culture began to view the world very much differently than the Hebrews. Around 200 BCE the Greeks began to move south causing a coming together of the Greek and Hebrew culture. This was a very tumultuous time as the two vastly different cultures collided.

Over the following 400 years the battle raged until finally the Greek culture won and virtually eliminated all traces of the Ancient Hebrew culture. The Greek culture then in turn, influenced all following cultures including the Roman and European cultures. Our own American culture and even the Modern Hebrew culture in Israel today are strongly influenced by the Greek culture.

As 21st Century Americans with a strong Greek thought influence, we read the Hebrew Bible as if a 21st Century American had written it. In order to understand the Ancient Hebrew culture in which the Bible was written in, we must examine some of the differences between Hebrew and Greek thought. There are many differences between Hebrew and Greek thought, but here we will confine our focus on those differences that impact the interpretation of words.

Abstract vs. concrete thought

Greek thought views the world through the mind (abstract thought). Ancient Hebrew thought views the world through the senses (concrete thought).

Concrete thought is the expression of concepts and ideas in ways that can be seen, touched, smelled, tasted and/or heard. All five of the senses are used when speaking, hearing, writing and reading the Hebrew language. An example of this can be found in Psalms 1:3; "He is like a *tree* planted by *streams of water*, which yields its *fruit* in season, and whose *leaf* does not *wither*". In this passage the author expresses his thoughts in concrete terms such as; tree, streams of water, fruit and leaf.

Abstract thought is the expression of concepts and ideas in ways that cannot be seen, touched, smelled, tasted or heard. Abstract thought is a foreign concept to the Ancient Hebrew mind. Examples of Abstract thought can be found in Psalms 103:8; "The LORD is *compassionate* and *gracious*, Slow to *anger*, abounding in *love*". The words compassion, grace, anger and love are all abstract words, ideas that cannot be experienced by the senses. Why do we find these abstract words in a passage of concrete thinking Hebrews? Actually, these are abstract English words used to translate the original Hebrew concrete words. The translators often translate this way because the original Hebrew makes no sense when literally translated into English.

Let us take one of the above abstract words to demonstrate the translation from a concrete Hebrew word to an abstract English word. Anger, an abstract word, is actually the Hebrew word אף / awph which literally means "nose", a concrete word. When one is very angry, he begins to breath hard and the nostrils begin to flare. A Hebrew sees anger as "the flaring of the nose (nostrils)". If the translator literally translated the above passage "slow to nose", the English reader would not understand.

Appearance vs. Functional Description

Greek thought describes objects in relation to its appearance. Hebrew thought describes objects in relation to its function.

A Greek description of a common pencil would be; "it is yellow and about eight inches long". A Hebrew description of the pencil would be related to its function such as "I write words with it". Notice that the Hebrew description uses the verb "write" while the Greek description uses the adjectives "yellow" and "long". Because of Hebrew's form of functional descriptions, verbs are used much more frequently then adjectives.

To our Greek way of thinking a deer and an oak are two very different objects and we would never describe them in the same way. The Hebrew word for both of these objects is איל / ayil because the functional description of these two objects are identical to the Ancient Hebrews, therefore, the same Hebrew word is used for both.

The Hebraic definition of איל is "a strong leader". A deer stag is one of the most powerful animals of the forest and is seen as "a strong leader" among the other animals of the forest. The wood of the oak tree is very hard compared to other trees and is seen as a "strong leader" among the trees of the forest.

Notice the two different translations of the Hebrew word איל in Psalms 29:9. The NASB and KJV translates it as *"The voice of the LORD makes the <u>deer</u> to calve"* while the NIV translates it as *"The voice of the LORD twists the <u>oaks</u>"*. The literal translation of this verse in Hebrew thought would be; *"The voice of the LORD makes the strong leaders turn "*.

When translating the Hebrew into English, the Greek thinking translator will give a Greek description to this word for the Greek thinking reader, which is why we have two different ways of translating this verse. This same word "ayil" is also translated as a "ruler" (a strong leader of men) in 2 Kings 24.15.

Passive vs. Active Nouns

Greek nouns are words that refer to a person, place or thing. Hebrew nouns refer to the action of a person place or thing.

The Hebrews are active people and their vocabulary reflects this lifestyle. The Greek culture recognizes words such as knee and gift as nouns, which by themselves impart no action. But, in Hebrew, just as in most Ancient languages[26], there is no distinction between nouns and verbs, all words are related to action. The Greek mind designates a knee and a gift as inanimate nouns unrelated in meaning. The Hebrew mind sees the knee (ברך / berak) as "the knee that bends" and a gift (ברכה / berakah) as "what is brought with a bent knee".

Even the Hebrew nouns for father and mother are descriptive of action. The Hebrew word for father is אב / av and literally means "the one who gives strength to the family" and mother אם / em means "the one that binds the family together".

When we read the Ancient texts of the Hebrew Bible we must remember that the words used are related to the Ancient Hebrew culture and thought. We need, therefore, to suppress our Western Greek minds, leaving them for reading the Modern classics.

---

[26] Giorgio Fano, <u>The Origins and Nature of Language</u> (Indiana University Press, Bloomington, 1992) 66

Three - Reconstructing the Original Hebrew Alphabet

The Ancient Hebrew letters form the foundation to the Ancient Hebrew language and a thorough study of these letters is essential to understanding the cultural background to the words they form. The process of reconstructing the original Hebrew alphabet is similar to the field of archeology, which digs down to hidden depths to determine the origins, culture or way of life of Ancient civilizations. As artifacts are found, they are compared to artifacts of other cultures and other time periods to determine the distinctive characteristics of the culture and civilization. When studying Ancient alphabets, one digs down into the depths of time and compares the artifacts of pictographic and non-pictographic scripts to determine dates, meaning and sound.

Letter Characteristics

We usually associate two characteristics for each letter, a form and a sound, as in the first letter of our alphabet whose form is "A" and has the sound "a". The Ancient Hebrew alphabet has four characteristics: form, sound, name and meaning.

1. Pictographic (form) -- The original letter is pictographic, meaning it represents a picture of something, such as the pictograph ⟅⟆ representing a mouth.

2. Mnemonic (meaning) -- The mnemonic meaning of a pictograph is the extended meanings related to the pictograph[27]. For example, the pictograph ⟅⟆, is a picture of a mouth, and has the extended mnemonic meanings of speak, blow and open. These mnemonic meanings most often are related to the pictograph by their function rather than appearance.

3. Syllabic (name) -- Each pictograph is associated with a single syllable of two consonants. This syllable is also the name of the pictograph. The name of the pictograph ⟅⟆ is "p*e*h"[28] and is also the Hebrew word for "mouth".

4. Phonetic (sound) -- The first letter of the syllabic name provides a singular sound for the purpose of forming words and sentences. The phonetic value of the pictograph ⟅⟆ / p*e*h is "p".

---

[27] Giorgio Fano, <u>The Origins and Nature of Language</u> (Bloomington: Indiana University Press, 1992) 20.

[28] When translating the Hebrew into English, it is often necessary to add vowels. These added vowels will be italicized.

Reconstruction of the Alphabet

By applying the below methods, the original Hebrew alphabet can be reconstructed with a fair amount of accuracy. Over time the fields of archeology, and their discoveries of artifacts and Ancient inscriptions, and anthropology, and their discoveries in linguistics and culture, may contribute additional information about the Ancient Hebrews to bring us even closer to the original.

Form

The original form of the letter is pictographic, meaning it represents a picture. For example, the picture ⟨⟩ is the form of a letter representing a mouth.

1. Comparison of Semitic scripts - Each letter of the Semitic cultures are carefully compared and arranged according to time and sub group. This historical chart can then be used to follow the progression of script evolution from one culture to the next throughout their written history. These charts can be seen in appendix "C".

2. Names of the pictographs - Each Hebrew pictograph have a name directly related to the picture. For example, the name of the pictograph "דּ" is "דלת" (dalet) which means "door" revealing the identity of the picture as that of a door. Just as scripts evolve, so do their names. Occasionally, Modern Hebrew names will no longer reflect the actual picture, but other languages do. For example, the word gimel (meaning a camel)[29] is now assigned to ⅃ with no apparent connection. The Arabic

---

[29] This Hebrew word means camel and has caused some confusion where this pictograph has been interpreted as a picture of a camel.

language has retained the original name of "gam" as has the Greek, "gamma".

3. Progression of letter evolution - By following the progression of each letters evolutionary process we see some common changes in the letters. For example, most of the pictographs were oriented in a horizontal position, but around 1000 BCE they shifted to a vertical orientation. This can help to fill in missing evolutionary changes.

4. Ancient Hebrew culture - The Ancient Hebrew language is very closely related to their lifestyle. Many times the Hebrew culture will reveal the meaning of the picture. For example, the pictograph ᴌ is named "beyt", meaning house. The connection between the pictograph and name is lost without knowledge of the Ancient houses made of tents, as the pictograph is a perfect representation of the floor plan of the tent.

Name

Just as the pictograph of a letter evolves over time, the names of the letter occasionally evolve or on rare occasion replaced. The name of the pictograph ⌒ is peh and is also the Hebrew word for "mouth".

1. Pictograph - What the pictograph represents is the first clue to what the name of the letter is. For example, the letter ⌒ is an eye. The Hebrew word for an eye is עִין (ayin) and is the Modern name for this letter.

2. Original Hebrew language - As will be demonstrated later, the original Hebrew language consisted of Parent and Child Roots while many of the three-letter roots, called adopted roots, were formed at a later time. From this we can conclude that any letter, whose Modern name is an adopted root, is not the original name of the letter. Interestingly, all but five Modern names are a parent or Child Root word.

3. Names of the letters of other cultures using the Hebrew alphabet - The names for each letter is usually transferred from one culture to another with either a slight change or no change at all. When there is a difference, the names are compared to determine the more original name.

Sound

Each letter represents a singular sound that is used to form words. For example the ⌐ (P) and 𝄐 (H) form the word PH (peh).

1. The name of the letter - The first letter of the name gives the phonetic value of the pictograph. For example, the name of the pictograph ⌐ is "pey" and has the phonetic value of "p".

2. The sound other cultures apply to the Hebrew alphabet - In most cases, the same sound is carried through the different culture. For example the ⌐ in its various forms through the different cultures all assign this letter a phonetic value of "P".

3. A unique sound for each letter - In the Modern Hebrew alphabet, two letters are silent (א and ע), two letters are assigned the "T" sound (ט and ת), and two letters are assigned the "S" sound (ס and שׁ). It is more likely that the original Hebrew alphabet did not waste letters by duplicating sound or using them as silent.

4. Vowels - All of the letters in the Hebrew alphabet are consonants. Some of these letters doubled as vowels much like the "Y" in the Roman alphabet, which can be a consonant as in the word "yellow", or a vowel as in the word "fly".

Meaning

The meaning of a letter is related to the picture[30] the form of the letter represents. These meanings are then a part of the meaning of the words, which use these letters.

1. The name of the letter - The name of the letter is a Hebrew word with meaning and usually more than one. For example the name of the letter ⌒ is "peh" and can mean mouth, speak, blow or edge.

Appendix "A" provides a detailed view of the reconstruction of the pictographic, mnemonic, syllabic and phonetic attributes of each Hebrew letter. Appendix "D" is a detailed chart of the Modern and Ancient Hebrew alphabet.

---

[30] Giorgio Fano, <u>The Origins and Nature of Language</u> (Bloomington: Indiana University Press, 1992) 20.

Four - Hebrew Prefixes

The idea of the form of a letter as providing meaning is foreign to our understanding of the purpose of the alphabet. In this chapter we are going to look at five Prefixes that are commonly added to Hebrew words; ⊔/B, ∪/L, ᴡ/M, Y/W and ⚨/H. These examples will demonstrate the relationship between the pictographs of each letter, their cultural understanding and their application in the Hebrew language.

⊔ The nomadic Hebrews lived in tents, and this letter is a representation of the tent. The door is in front (top left of the picture) and a wall (middle of the picture) separates the men's side (left side) from the women's side (right side). Since the family resides inside the tent, this letter means "in". When the letter ⊔/B is placed in front of a word such as ⌐⊓⋎/erets (land), we have ⌐⊓⋎⊔/be'arets (in a[31] land).

∪ The Hebrew shepherd always carried a staff and was used to move the sheep toward the destination. This letter means "to" or "toward". When the letter ∪/L is placed in front of the word ⌐⊓⋎, we have ⌐⊓⋎∪ (to a land).

---

[31] Hebrew does not express the idea "a" or "an", rather it is implied.

ᴀᴀᴀ This letter is a picture of water and can also mean the flowing water in man and animals (blood). Blood is seen as the passing down a line from one generation to another. When this letter is prefixed to a word it means "from" in the sense of coming out of someone or something. When the letter ᴀᴀ/M is placed in front of the word ⟨land⟩, we have ⟨me'erets⟩/me'erets (from *a* land).

Y This letter is a picture of a tent peg used to secure the tent, or a nail used to attach things together. When this letter is prefixed to a word it means "and" in the sense of adding things together. When the letter Y/W is placed in front of the word ⟨land⟩, we have ⟨ve'erets⟩/ve'erets (and land).

ᵠ This letter is a picture of a mans arms raised or extended toward someone or something as if saying "behold, look at this. When this letter is prefixed to a word it means "the" as in identifying someone or something in particular When the letter ᵠ/H is placed in front of the word ⟨land⟩, we have ⟨ha'erets⟩/ha'erets (the land).

Five - The Root System of Hebrew

The Hebrew language uses a root system for its vocabulary. The root system is like a tree where the leaves (words) come from the branches (Child Root). The Branches come from the trunk (Parent Root) and the trunk comes out of the roots (letters).

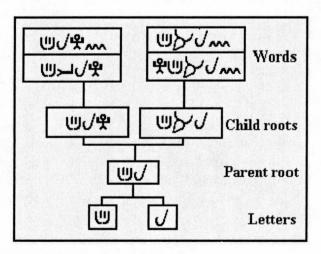

Figure 19 Hebrew root word systems

Parent Roots

When two letters/pictographs are put together, a Parent Root word is formed. When the ⌂ (bet, a house) is combined with the ↖ (nun, a seed which continues the next generation) the Parent Root ⌐ (pronounced ben[32]) is formed. The two letters of this root have the combined meaning of "the house of seeds" or "the seeds that continue the house/family" and are usually translated simply as "son".

Another example is the Parent Root ⌐ (shaph)[33]. The ⌐ is a picture of the two front teeth meaning "sharp". The ⌐ is a mouth. This Parent Root means "a sharp mouth" or simply "a serpent" whose sharp fangs are in the mouth.

Hebrew word structure, as will be seen later, often requires a three consonant root; therefore the second consonant in the Parent Root is duplicated to turn the two consonant Parent Root into a three consonant root. The meaning of this derivative from the Parent Root is usually identical in meaning to the original Parent Root. As in our example above, the second letter ⌐ is doubled, forming the root ⌐ (shaphaph), also meaning "serpent".

Child Roots

Of the 22 letters of the Hebrew alphabet, 4 double as consonants and vowels[34], the 𝒴 (a), ✿ (e), Υ (o and u) and ⌐ (i).

A Child Root is formed by adding one of the consonant/vowels as a prefix (in front), a suffix (at the

---

[32] Hebrew is written from right to left.
[33] The Biblical word for serpent is "shaphaph" a lengthened form of the parent root "shaph".
[34] Ernst Ettisch, The Hebrew Vowels and Consonants (Brookline Village Ma: Branden Publishing Co., 1987) 87. William R. Harper PH. D., Elements of Hebrew (New York: Charles Scribner's Sons, 1895) 17. E. Kautzsch, Gesenius' Hebrew Grammar (London: Oxford, 1910) 35.

end) or an infix (in the middle) to the Parent Root. While the Parent Root represents a concrete subject with a wide range of mnemonic meanings, the purpose of the Child Root is to separate out the various mnemonic meanings of the Parent Root. Therefore, all the Child Roots formed from the Parent Root are directly related in meaning to the Parent Root. Below are the Child Roots, as found in the Biblical text, formed from the Parent Root ᴠᴌ / בל / b*al*, which has the generic meaning of "flow", demonstrating the close relationship to each other and the Parent Root.

ᴠᴌᴘᵞ	a.b.l	- wilt: a flowing away of life
ᴠᴌᴘᵠ	h.b.l	- empty: flowing out of contents
ᴠᵠᴘ	b.h.l	- panic: a flowing of the insides
ᵠᴠᴘ	b.l.h	- aged: a flowing away of youth
ᴠᵞᴘ	b.w.l	- flood: a heavy flowing of water
ᴠᴌᴘᴊ	y.b.l	- stream: a flowing of water

By placing the consonant letter ᴋ (nun) within the Parent Root, a new type of Child Root is formed. This Child Root is very closely related to the parent. For example, the Parent Root ᴑᵞ / אַף / aph means nose or the flaring of the nostrils as when angry. The Child Root ᴑᴋᵞ / אנף / anaph also means angry.

Adopted Roots

There are two forms of adopted roots that were probably derived at a later time through the evolution of the language[35] or adopted from another Shemitic language.

---

[35] Approximately 80% of all the words found in the Bible are derived from the parent or child root words, while the remaining 20% are derived from the combination roots. These significantly smaller numbers of combination roots indicate that these roots have a

The first is formed by adding a third consonant to a Parent Root forming a new root more specific in meaning than the parent, such as the examples below;

𐤓𐤐	p.r	- Parent Root meaning break
𐤇𐤓𐤐	p.r.c	- break forth
𐤊𐤓𐤐	p.r.k	- break apart
𐤔𐤓𐤐	p.r.s	- break in pieces
𐤒𐤓𐤐	p.r.q	- break off
𐤑𐤓𐤐	p.r.ts	- break open

The second type of adopted root appears to be a three consonant root that evolved from the Parent Root into a new word with a similar sound. As a language evolves, words exchange letters for similar sounding letters and additional letters are added. For example the word 𐤓𐤓𐤊/derek meaning "road" probably evolved out of 𐤇𐤓/rach meaning "path".

Words

The most common words are those derived directly from the parent, Child Root or adopted root. For example the word כהן/kohen, meaning "priest", comes directly from the Child Root כהן.

Adding specific letters in specific places within the root word forms other words. Some of the most common additions to the original root found are:

1. a 𐤌/מ/m or 𐤕/ת/t added to the front or back of the root word

---

relatively late origin and are not part of the original Hebrew vocabulary.

2. a 𐤄/ה/h, 𐤅𐤕/ות/wt or 𐤅𐤍/ון/wn added to the back of the root word

3. a 𐤅/ו/w or 𐤉/י/ee added in front of the last letter of the root word.

Benefit of studying words from a common root

As all the roots and words, which are derived from the Parent Root, are related in meaning to the Parent Root[36], we can compare their meanings[37] to form a clearer picture of the original meaning of the Parent Root. The pictographs of the Parent Root will also help us to determine the original meaning of this Parent Root. Once the meaning of the Parent Root is determined, this will in turn help us to better define the roots and words derived from the parent. Let us use the Parent Root 𐤋𐤊/לך[38]/l.k as an example;

Root	Word	Meaning
Parent	𐤋𐤊	Walk
Child	𐤄𐤋𐤊	Walk
	𐤄𐤋𐤉𐤊	Step
	𐤄𐤋𐤊𐤄	March
	𐤌𐤋𐤊𐤄	Walking
	𐤌𐤄𐤋𐤊𐤅𐤄	Walk
Child	𐤉𐤋𐤊	Walk

The original pictographs of the Parent Root are 𐤋𐤊 and are the pictures of a *shepherd staff* and the *palm of the hand*. While these pictographs can have a wide range of

---

[36] Horowitz, 22.

[37] The more roots and words available, the clearer the picture of the parent root will be.

[38] The Kaph is written as ך when at the end of a word and a כ when in a word.

meaning due to the various mnemonic understandings, the words that are derived from it have the meanings of walk, step and march. Therefore, we can understand the pictographs to mean "to carry a **staff** in the **palm** for walking".

Reconstructing the Parent Roots

The meanings of the Parent Roots provide the foundation for the meaning of all the Child Root that are formed out of it. These Parent Roots were generic in meaning whereas the Child Roots derived from them become more specific in meaning. For instance, the Parent Root "בר" (BR) means, grain, but can also mean any product of the grain, such as; fat, meat, fowl, soap and clean. The Child Roots carry the more specific meaning such as; "אבר" (ABR) meaning, fowl; "ברא" (BRA) meaning, fat and meat; "בהר" (BHR) meaning, soap and clean; and "ברה" (BRH) meaning, grain.

A working dictionary of the Parent Roots is beneficial to word studies and Biblical understanding. Two problems arise when working with Parent Roots. First, not all of the Parent Roots have survived to this day and second, those that have survived have often become specific in meaning, losing the original generic meaning. While the entire Parent Root system cannot be achieved completely, there are techniques to reconstructing it for the purpose of Biblical studies.

Methods for reconstructing the original Parent Root

1. Pictographs - The pictographs provide the basic meaning of the root as demonstrated previously.

2. Words - By comparing all of the words that are derived from the Parent Root, the generic meaning of the Parent Root can be found. For instance, "בר" (BR) means, grain; "ברבר" (BRBR) means, fowl; and "ברר" (BRR) means, clean or pure. The more words available, the clearer the definition of the Parent Root will be.

3. Child Roots - All of the words derived from a child root help to reconstruct the original meaning of the Child Root in the same manner as mentioned above for the Parent Root. All of the Child Root definitions will then help to reconstruct the generic meaning of the Parent Root.

4. Sister Languages - Semitic languages such as Ugarit, Aramaic, Phoenician, Moabite, etc. are closely related to Hebrew and many times the words are identical. The words from these languages can assist with the reconstruction of the Child and Parent Roots.

While the pictographs, words and Child Roots contribute to reconstructing the Parent Root, the Parent Root will in turn assist with defining the Child Roots and Words. The use of this Root System of the Hebrew language is beneficial to finding the correct Hebraic meaning to words by looking at the bigger picture of related words and roots. This can be very beneficial when attempting to translate obscure or frequently used words. Translating Hebrew words, which are only used once or twice in the Biblical texts, are very difficult to define due to a lack of context. But, when using the root system of Hebrew, we can use the many related words derived from the same Parent Root to assist with defining the word.

Even if a Parent Root is not found in the Biblical text, or other related language, it can still be reconstructed by using the above methods and still be useful for defining the other words and roots formed out of it.

Appendix "E" is a dictionary of the Ancient Hebrew Parent Roots. This dictionary gives the cultural background and its relationship to the Child Roots, which are derived from them. Appendix "F" cross-references the Strong's Dictionary numbering system to the Ancient Hebrew Dictionary numbering system.

Six - Word Studies

The purpose of this book is to provide the reader with the tools and resources to read the Bible with a Hebraic understanding and see the text through the eyes of the Ancient Hebrew who wrote it.

Let us now put all this "technical" information to work by looking at a passage through Hebraic eyes.

God

> "*God Most High, Creator of heaven and earth.*" (Genesis 14.22)

We will examine two words within this sentence, God and Creator. Both of these words are abstract words from Greek thought. Our goal is to find the tangible concrete Hebraic context of these words that will reveal the heart of God the Creator

The Hebrew word translated as "God" is אל / al and is a Parent Root word. The Ancient pictographs for this root are 𐤋𐤀. The first picture (remember Hebrew is read from right to left) is an ox head representative of power because of his great strength. The second is a shepherd's staff and is representative of authority as well as a yoke[39].

---

[39] Isaiah 9.4, through Hebrew parallelism, describes the yoke as a "staff on the shoulders". The wooden staff used by the shepherd to guide the sheep toward a location. The yoke, also made of wood, was

A team of oxen yoked together pulled a cart or plow. To train the younger oxen, an older more experienced ox as the leader was yoked to the younger. The Hebraic meaning of אֵל / al is a "powerful leader". The Ancient Hebrews saw themselves yoked to God who taught them how to walk a proper life.

Creator

The second word, Creator, is the Hebrew word קָנֵה qaneh derived from the Parent Root קֵן / qen meaning a nest. The pictographs for this word are ⌐-⊙. The first pictograph is the sun at the horizon where light is gathered. The mnemonic meaning of this letter is a gathering together. The second picture is a seed. The combining these letters mean a "gathering together for the seeds". Before the bird lays her eggs she gathers material together to build a nest. The Child Root ⊙-⌐-⌡ / קָנָה has the meaning of acquiring the materials for the nest. The Ancient Hebrews saw God as a bird[40] that builds a nest, the heavens and the land, for his children.

The Hebraic understanding of this verse is that God brought together the heavens and the earth as the nest for his children he could nurture and care for them as a mother and teach and guide them into truth by yoking them to himself.

---

also used to guide the oxen toward a location. Both the shepherd's staff and the yoke perform the same function.
[40] See Deuteronomy 32.9-12

Voice

Let us look at Deuteronomy 5.22 as another example of how the Hebraic understanding of words reveals the heart of God.

> "*These are the commandments the LORD proclaimed in a loud voice to your whole assembly there on the mountain from out of the fire.*"

Two words in this passage, assembly and voice, come from the same Parent Root ◡-ⵁ- / קל / qal. We have previously looked at these two pictographs in this chapter. The first letter is the sun at the horizon meaning, to gather. The second is the shepherd's staff. Combined they have the meaning of "to gather to the staff of the shepherd".

The shepherd carried a staff as a tool to lead and guide the sheep as well as to discipline and protect them. The staff is a sign of his authority over the sheep. When the shepherd calls the flock, they recognize his voice and gather to him. The Hebrew word ◡Y-ⵁ- / קול / qol (translated as "voice" in our passage above) is "the voice of the shepherd". The Hebrew word ◡⚹-ⵁ- / קהל / qahal (translated as "assembly" above) is "the gathering of the sheep to the voice of the shepherd".

The Ancient Hebraic understanding of this verse is that God is the shepherd who will teach and protect his sheep and when he calls them they come to him as his flock.

Ancient Hebrew Words

By examining the titles of family members through the pictographic letters that form the words, we can better understand the Hebraic definition of these words.

Father

The first letter is the ᕗ/al, a picture of an ox. As the ox is strong, the letter also has the meaning of strong. The second letter, ᒲ/bet, is the picture of the tent or house where the family resides.

ᒲᕗ: One who gives strength to the house

❖❖❖❖❖❖

Mother

This word also begins with the letter ᕗ/al, meaning "strong". The second letter is the ᨓ/mah, meaning water. The two letters give us the meaning of "strong water". The Hebrews made glue by boiling animal skins in water. As the skin broke down a sticky thick liquid formed at the surface of the water. This thick liquid was removed and used as a binding agent - "strong water".

ᨓᕗ: One who glues/binds the family together

❖❖❖❖❖❖

Brother

This word also begins with ᕗ/al, meaning "strong". The second letter is the ᨑ/hhets, a picture of a wall. These letters give us the meaning "strong wall" or "strong barrier". The English concept of a wall is descriptive of anything with a tall vertical appearance. The Hebrew concept of a wall is any barrier, no matter the construction.

ᴥ: One who acts as a strong barrier to protect the family

Son

This word begins with the ⌂/bet, meaning "tent" or the "family" which resides in it. The second letter is the ↙/nun, the picture of a seed. The seed is a new generation of life that will grow and produce a new generation.

ᴅ: One who continues the family line

Seven - Hebrew origins of English

As we have discussed, the Modern Hebrew alphabet is derived from the Ancient Hebrew pictographs. The Romans in turn adopted the Greek alphabet, also derived from the Ancient Hebrew pictographs, for the Latin alphabet, from which our English alphabet comes. Indirectly, our own alphabet is derived from the Ancient Hebrew pictographs. Below is the Ancient Hebrew alphabet, as it appeared around 1000 BCE[41] (fig. 20).

Figure 20   The Ancient Hebrew alphabet c. 1000 BCE

When the above alphabet is reversed[42], as the Greeks, who adopted the Ancient Hebrew alphabet, wrote from left to right, we can see a very close resemblance to our English alphabet (fig. 21).

---

[41] The alephbet is read from right to left.

[42] Most Ancient inscriptions were written on stone using a hammer and chisel. The hammer was held with the left hand, causing a right to left direction of inscribing. When ink came into use, the direction of writing often shifted to a left to right direction to prevent the hand from smearing the ink.

ᐊᏔ<ᐅᖵᚻᒉ Z ᚻᑌᔍᛕ\ ᛗᛆ ᚍᐤᒉᖴᖳᏢᴡ†
A B C D E F Z H   I K L M N X O P   Q R S T

Figure 21   The Ancient Hebrew alphabet c. 1000 BCE (mirror image)

A surprising number of our English words are derived from Hebrew. As an example, the Hebrew word פרי / periy, meaning fruit, is a derivative of the Parent Root פר / par. The English words **p**ear, **p**rune, **p**ersimmon and a**p**ricot, all fruits, are derived from the פר / par root.

Through the evolution of language, it is common for similar sounds to replace the original sound. The "r" and "l" sounds are often interchanged as both are vocal[43] consonants and can be pronounced for a prolonged time. The English fruit words app**l**e and p**l**um, are also derived from the פר / par root with the "r" exchanged for an "l" sound.

Another common sound change is made with the lips such as the "b", "p", "v" and "f". The English fruit words **b**erry and **f**ruit, are also derived from the פר / par root with the "p" exchanged for a "b" and "f" sound. In addition, letters will some times change position such as the fruit word g**r**a**p**e and **r**i**p**e.

Another example is the Parent Root בר / bar, meaning grain. From this root several English words are derived and related to "grain", such as: **b**arley (a grain); **b**read and **b**eer (products of grains); **b**oar, **b**ird and **b**ear

---

[43] As opposed to the frictives like the "s, sh" sounds which are given sound by blowing air through the mouth.

(animals fattened on grains); and **barn** (a storage place for grains).

Below is a very small list of Hebrew words practically identical in pronunciation and meaning to English.

Hebrew	Pronunciation	Meaning	English
אִישׁ	eesh	each	each
נוד	nod	nod	nod
גמל	gamel	camel	camel
נפל	naphal	fall	fall
עבר	over	over	over
אלף	eleph	bull	elephant
טל	tal	tall	tall
אש	eysh	fire	ash
כפר	caphar	cover	cover
קול	qol	voice	call
ספיר	saphiyr	sapphire	sapphire
שק	saq	sack	sack
תור	tur	travel	tour
תף	taph	beat	tap
ארץ	erets	land	earth
צד	tsad	side	side
סר	sar	prince	sir
סך	sak	shack	shack
שדה	sadeh	field	sod
מוק	moq	mock	mock
לק	laq	lick	lick
לב	lev	heart	love
כסה	kasah	cover	case

Conclusion

Contained within this book are the tools you will need to begin searching the pictographic meanings of Hebrew words. Other resource materials, which you will find beneficial in your word studies, are dictionaries such as "Vines Expository Dictionary of Biblical Words" or "Strong's Hebrew Dictionary". Bible Encyclopedias are another valuable resource for learning about the culture and lifestyle of the Ancient Hebrews.

It is the hope of the author that others will discover the value and joy of studying the Ancient Hebrew language, alphabet and Biblical Text. The Seminaries and Universities emphasize the Greek language, practically ignoring the language and culture of the Ancient Hebrews. There is very little research and study being done in this area of linguistic study at this time, but hopefully this will change in the future.

For further information or questions on the Ancient Hebrew language and alphabet, please visit our web site at:

The Ancient Hebrew Research Center
http://www.ancient-hebrew.org

Appendix A - Ancient Hebrew Alphabet Reconstruction

Below is the process of reconstructing the original characteristics of each Hebrew letter using the methods previously outlined.

ϫ Al

Pictographic (form): All sources agree that the original form for this letter is ϫ, an ox head.

Mnemonic (meaning): *Muscle* -- the ox is the strongest of the livestock animals; *Yoke* -- the ox is placed in a yoke for pulling a load or plowing; *Chief* -- an older experienced ox, as the leader, was often yoked to a younger ox to teach him; *Oak tree* -- the strongest of the woods; *Ram* -- the strong leader of the flock; *Stag* -- the strong leader of the forest; *Fat tail* -- the strong part of the sheep; *Pillar, arch* -- the strong members which support a building.

Syllabic (name): The Modern Hebrew, Greek and Arabic name for this letter is aleph. The original two-letter name must have evolved to its present three-letter name long ago. This is the only pictograph for which the original two-letter name cannot be found. We then turn to the culture of the Ancient Hebrews and sister cultures to find the original name. Many Near Eastern cultures worshipped the god "אל / el or al", depicted as a bull in their carvings of the god. When Israel formed an image of God at Mount Sinai they chose a calf (young bull). This evidence shows that the word "אל / el" was understood to be a bull.

Phonetic (sound): In Modern Hebrew as well as Arabic, this letter is silent but did have an "a" sound when the Greek language adopted it. This letter was originally a vowel and most likely an "ah" sound.

⊔ Beyt

Pictographic (form): The Hebrew word beyt means "house" or "tent". There are various suggestions to the original form of this letter including ⊓, ◻, ⊓ and ⊔. The picture ⊔ is a perfect representation of the nomadic tent which was divided into two sections, a men's and women's, with the entrance at the front of the tent in the men's section and an entrance from the men's to the women's section.

Mnemonic (meaning): *Family* -- the residents of the tent; *Inside* -- the family that is inside the tent is of importance, not the structure itself.

Syllabic (name): Modern Hebrew (beyt), Greek (beta) and Arabic (beyt) agree with the original name of בת / bet, meaning, house or tent.

Phonetic (sound): The Modern sounds for this letter are "b" and "bh"[44] and are probably original.

⌐ Gam

Pictographic (form): The earliest known pictograph for this letter is ⌐ and is probably a picture of a foot similar to the Egyptian Hieroglyph ⌐.

Mnemonic (meaning): *Walk, Gather, Carry* -- the function of the foot; *Group* -- a gathering of people or things.

Syllabic (name): The Modern Hebrew name for this letter is gimel. The Greek (gamma) and Arabic (jeem) names for this letter, provide us with the original two letter name of גמ / gam meaning to gather.

Phonetic (sound): The Modern Hebrew and Greek agree that the letter is pronounced "g" while Arabic has the sound "j", a derivative of the sound "g".

---

[44] It is a common practice among Latin languages to add an "h" to a consonant to show a different sound, such as p-ph, c-ch, t-th, s-sh. In this case the bh is pronounced as a "v".

⊓ Dal

Pictographic (form): Ancient alphabet charts include two possibilities for the Ancient pictographic form for this letter, ⋈ (a fish -- "dahg" in Hebrew) and ⊓ (a picture of a tent door -- "dahl" or "delet" in Hebrew). The Modern name for this letter is dalet meaning a door indicating that the original form of the letter is the ⊓.

Mnemonic (meaning): *Dangle* -- the tent door hangs down from the horizontal pole as seen in the picture of the letter; *Movement* -- the door is used to move in and out or back and forth through the tent; *Weak, Poor* -- one who hangs his head down, as in poverty.

Syllabic (name): While the Modern Hebrew name for this letter is dalet (3 consonants), the Arabic name of דל / dal (the original 2 consonant root), meaning door, gives us the original two letter name.

Phonetic (sound): Hebrew (*d*alet), Greek (*d*elta) and Arabic (*d*al) agree that the sound for this letter is "d".

♀ Hey

Pictographic (form): Most all sources agree that the original picture is ♀, a man with his arms raised out as if pointing toward something.

Mnemonic (meaning): *Look* -- when one sees a great sight he throws his arms toward it and sighs saying "look at that"; *Reveal* -- a pointing to a sight to show to another; *Breath* -- as when sighing.

Syllabic (name): The Modern Hebrew (hey) and Arabic (hey) have retained the original two letter name of הא / hey meaning look.

Phonetic (sound): This letter originally had a consonant "h" sound, as retained in Modern Hebrew, as well as a vowel "e" sound as retained in the Greek.

Υ Waw

Pictographic (form): Ancient alphabet charts include two possibilities for the Ancient pictographic form for this letter, Υ and Ϙ. The Hebrew word vav / waw means a peg. The tent pegs were made of wood and may have been Y-shaped as in the first picture to prevent the rope from slipping off.

Mnemonic (meaning): *Add, Secure* -- the peg is used for securing or tying the tent or other items together.

Syllabic (name): The Modern Hebrew name for this letter is וו / vav, meaning peg, retaining the original two letter name.

Phonetic (sound): While the Modern pronunciation for this letter is "vav", the original sound for this letter was "w" and is retained in the Modern Arabic as "waw". This letter also doubled as a vowel with a "ow" and "uw" sound which Modern Hebrew has retained.

⊏ Zan

Pictographic (form): The most Ancient picture for this is ⊏, a picture of an unknown agricultural tool, probably a type of plow, hoe or sickle. The Egyptian hieroglyph ⌐ is very similar and is a hoe and may be the original form for this letter.

Mnemonic (meaning): *Harvest, food* -- from the cutting of the crops with the tool; *Fed, Fattened* -- from eating the crops; *Jar* -- for storing the harvested foods; *Broad* -- from the broad blade of the tool; *Paddle, Ear, Spade* -- from their broadness.

Syllabic (name): The Modern Hebrew name is זין / zayin, a derivative of the two letter word זן / zan, meaning crops, which is the original Greek name for this letter.

Phonetic (sound): Hebrew, Greek and Arabic agree that the sound for this letter is "z".

▥ Hhets

Pictographic (form): There are three possible Ancient pictographs for this letter, 웅, ⵣ and ▥. The first is apparently a string or cord. The second is a man with his arms extended and belongs to the fifth letter hey. The third is a nomadic tent wall, which is "hhets" in Hebrew. The two horizontal lines are the top and bottom and the four vertical lines being the poles. All the letters from 3,000 BCE to the present day in the Hebrew, Arabic Greek and their sister cultures have used a derivative of the third pictograph, the tent wall.

Mnemonic (meaning): *Outside, Inside* -- the function of the wall is to separate these two; *Half* -- a dividing into two parts; *Secular* -- what is outside; *Arrow, Slingstone* -- from their dividing of flesh

Syllabic (name): The Modern Hebrew name is חת / chet, meaning a string. A very similar word is חץ / hhets, meaning a wall, most likely the original name for this letter.

Phonetic (sound): The original sound for this letter is probably a guttural "hh" (as in the name Bach and the German word ich), as in Modern Hebrew and Arabic.

⊗ Thet

Picture: The oldest form of the original pictograph is ⊗, apparently a type of basket or container.

Mnemonic (meaning): *Store, Contain* -- baskets were used for storing foods, supplies and other necessities of the nomadic life; *Mud, Clay* -- a material for making baskets and other containers.

Syllabic (name): Modern Hebrew has retained the original two letter word טט / tet, meaning mud or clay, for the name of this letter.

Phonetic (sound): The 22nd letter of the Hebrew alphabet is a tav with a "t" sound. It is unlikely that the original Hebrew had two letters with the same sound. When the Greeks adopted the Hebrew alphabet the Hebrew tet became the Greek theta. Most likely the original sound for this letter is "th".

Appendix A – Alphabet Reconstruction

◝◟ Yad

Pictograph: The most Ancient form of the letter is ◝◟, an arm and hand.

Mnemonic (meaning): *Work, Make, Throw* -- from the function of the hand; Shout -- from the placing of the hands at the mouth for amplification; *Worship, Thanks* -- a giving of the hand as a gesture.

Syllabic (name): The Modern Hebrew name יוד / yud is a derivative of the two letter word יד / yad meaning "hand".

Phonetic (sound): The Modern Hebrew and Arabic sound for this letter is a "y". This letter also doubled as a vowel that can be seen from the Greek form of this letter, which is an iota with an "i", or "ee" sound.

Ⱳ Kaph

Pictographic (form): The Ancient form of this letter is Ⱳ, the open palm of a hand.

Mnemonic (meaning): *Sole* -- the palm of the foot; *Bend, Curve* -- the shape of the open palm; *Bowl, Palm Branch* -- from the curved palm shape; *Tame, Subdue* -- from the bending of the will, as an open hand signifies submission.

Syllabic (name): Modern Hebrew, Greek and Arabic, agree that the original name for this letter is כף / kaph, meaning, palm.

57

Phonetic (sound): Modern Hebrew, Greek and Arabic agree that the sound for this letter is "k" and a guttural "kh" (as in the name Bach or the German word ich).

∪ Lam

Pictographic (form): The Ancient picture is ∪, a shepherd's staff.

Mnemonic (meaning): *To, Toward* -- the staff was used to push, or pull one of the flock in a direction; *Authority* -- the staff as a sign of the shepherd's authority; *Yoke* -- a staff on the shoulders of the oxen for directing; *Bind, Tie* -- from the fastening of the yoke.

Syllabic (name): The Modern Hebrew name for this letter is למד / lamed, meaning staff, and is similar to the Greek name of lamda. The Arabic name is לם / lam retaining the original two letter word.

Phonetic (sound): Hebrew, Greek and Arabic agree that the sound for this letter is "l".

∿ Mah

Pictographic (form): The Ancient picture is ∿, waves of water.

Mnemonic (meaning): *Sea* -- a large body of water; *Chaos* -- from the storms of the sea; *Mighty, Massive* -- from the size of the sea; *Who, What, When, Where, Why, How* -- the sea is the place of the unknown representing any unknown thing; *Blood, Grape Juice* -- as liquids.

Syllabic (name): The Hebrew letter מם / mem is from the word מים / mayim meaning waters and is the plural form of the two letter word מה / mah.

Phonetic (sound): Hebrew, Greek and Arabic agree that the sound for this letter is "m".

ꞥ Nun

Pictographic (form): The Ancient picture is ꞥ, a seed sprout.

Mnemonic (meaning): *Continue*, *Perpetuate* -- The seed perpetuates or continues the plant generation after generation; *Offspring*, *Heir* -- the perpetuation of the father through his children.

Syllabic (name): The Modern Hebrew and Arabic name for this letter is נן / nun meaning to continue or perpetuate.

Phonetic (sound): Hebrew, Greek and Arabic agree that the sound for this letter is "n".

⚔ Sin

Pictographic (form): The four possibilities for the original form for this letter are ⌖ (a fish), ⟨ (possibly a thorn), ⊞ (possibly a window) or ⚔ (a thorn). All the letters from 3,000 BCE to the present day in the Hebrew, Arabic Greek and their sister cultures have used a derivative of ⚔ suggesting that this is the original letter.

Mnemonic (meaning): *Shield* -- thorn bushes were used by the shepherd to build a wall (shield) made to enclose his flock during the night to protect them from predators; *Flock* -- as protected in the wall of thorns; *Pierce, Sharp* -- from the sharpness of the thorn; *Warrior* -- as a wall of sharp weapons for protection; *Boot* -- as protection from thorns; *Hate* -- as a piercing of the heart)

Syllabic (name): Of all the letters this is the most difficult to reconstruct due to the limited archeological and textual support. The Modern Hebrew name for this letter is סמח / samech, with no apparent connection to a two letter word or to the original picture of this letter. The Arabic alphabet does not have this letter and the Greek name for the letter is ksi. The 21st letter of the Hebrew alphabet (ש) has two names and sounds, שִׁן / Shin (sh) and שִׂן / Sin (s). All the words using the sin are related in meaning to the words using a samech in the same place as the sin. It is possible that the original name for the samech was סן / sin, meaning thorn, and later was divided into the samech and שִׂן / sin (which then became associated with the שִׁן / shin).

Phonetic (sound): The original sound for this letter must be an "s" to which the samech and sin both agree. The Greek sound for the letter is "ks", similar to the "s".

◎ Ghan

Pictographic (form): The Ancient picture is ◎, an eye.

Mnemonic (meaning): *Watch, Pay attention, Heed* -- as keeping a close eye on something; *Cover* -- as a shading of the eyes to remove the glare of the sun; *Furrow* --

formed between the eyes from squinting; Affliction, *Worry, Poor, Humble* -- one with a furrow between the eyes; *Occupation* -- one paying attention to the task; *Abode* -- as a place carefully watched; *Spring, Source* -- the eye of the landscape; *Ostrich, Owl* -- a bird that watches

Syllabic (name): The Modern Hebrew name for this letter is ayin. Arabic has two names for this letter, ayin and ghayin. The Greek name is "Omicron" (a definite name change by the Greeks).

Phonetic (sound): This letter is silent in Modern Hebrew. Arabic has two forms, the ayin, which is silent, and the ghayin with a "gh"[45] sound. The Egyptian hieratic alphabet also has a "ghayin" with a "gh" sound. When the Septuagint (Greek translation of the Hebrew Bible) transliterated place names such as פער to Pegor and עמרה to Gemorah, they attributed a "g" sound to the ayin indicating a sound similar to a "g" (since Greek does not have a "gh", a "g" would be the closest). The "gh" also served as a glottal stop, as in our English word bottle, where the "tt" is only slightly pronounced and in the Hebrew name בעל / ba'al where the ayin is used as a glottal stop. The gimel (ג / g) has been mistaken for the ghayin (ע / gh) in Hebrew. Both words גלל (g.l.l) and עלל (gh.l.l) mean "around" showing that the two letters were phonetically common.

⟳ Pey

Pictographic (form): There are several Canaanite pictographs believed to be this letter, none of which

---

45 Pronounced as an "ng" as in "ri<u>ng</u>".

resemble a mouth (the meaning of the name of the letter). The South Arabian and Egyptian pictograph is ⌐, and does look like a mouth. Most of the Hebrew, Arabic, Greek and their sister cultures use a pictograph similar to the ⌐.

Mnemonic (meaning): *Speak, Word, Blow* -- the function of the mouth; *Scatter* -- by blowing; *Edge* -- the lips as the edge of the mouth; *Sword, Beard* -- Things with edges; *Here, Region* -- a place with an edge

Syllabic (name): The Modern Hebrew, Arabic and Greek names agree with פה / peh, meaning mouth, as the original two letter name.

Phonetic (sound): Hebrew, Greek and Arabic agree that the sound for this letter is "p". This letter also has a "ph" sound in the Modern Hebrew and is probably an original sound as well.

⌒ᴧ Tsad

Pictographic (form): The three Ancient pictograph possibilities for this letter are ⵣ, ⌒⊃ and ⌒ᴧ. The word "tsad" means "side" as a man lying on his side and may be the meaning of the last two pictographs. The Hebrew, Arabic, Greek and their sister cultures use pictographs which closely resemble the last picture indicating that this was the original form of the letter.

Mnemonic (meaning): *Hunt, Chase* -- as one laying on his side or crouched in concealment; *Net, Snare* -- Tools of the hunter; *Fortress, Stronghold, Tower* -- a place to lay in wait; *Game* -- the meat of the hunt

Syllabic (name): The Modern Hebrew and Arabic name for this letter is tsade or tsad meaning side.

Phonetic (sound): Hebrew and Arabic agree that the sound for this letter is "ts".

⊖ Quph

Pictographic (form): Most of the pictographs used for this letter are Υ or something very similar. The South Arabian pictograph has a similar pictograph of Υ, possibly depicting the sun at the horizon (when rotated 90°, a common shift in Ancient letters). The original form of this letter was probably ⊖, reflecting the meaning of the Hebrew words derived from quph, meaning, "go around" and "revolution of the sun".

Mnemonic (meaning): *Sun* -- from its circles through the sky marking the times and seasons; *Horizon* -- from the rising and setting of the sun; *Condense* -- from the condensing of the light when the sun rises or sets; *Circle* -- from the arching of the sun in the sky; *Time* -- as a revolution of the sun

Syllabic (name): The Modern Hebrew and Arabic name for this letter is the parent root קֹף / quph meaning, circle or go around.

Phonetic (sound): Hebrew, Greek and Arabic agree that the sound for this letter is "q".

ᏒᏩ   Resh

Pictographic (form): The Ancient picture is ᏒᏩ, the head of a man.

Mnemonic (meaning): *Top, Beginning, First* -- as the top of the body; Chief -- the head of the tribe; *Rule* -- the role of the chief; *Needy, Poor* -- one in need of a ruling from the chief; *Possession, Inheritance* -- decided by the chief

Syllabic (name): The Modern Hebrew name for this letter is רש / resh, meaning head.

Phonetic (sound): Hebrew, Greek and Arabic agree that the sound for this letter is "r".

᥉᥊   Shin

Pictographic (form): The Ancient picture ᥉᥊ is the two front teeth.

Mnemonic (meaning): *Sharp, Press* -- the function of the teeth; *Cliff* -- as a tooth; *Ivory* -- the tusks of the elephant as teeth; *Two, duplicate, repeat, double, second, again* -- as the two front teeth

Syllabic (name): The Modern Hebrew and Arabic name for this letter is שן / Shin, meaning teeth.

Phonetic (sound): Hebrew and Arabic agree that the sound for this letter is "sh". Modern Hebrew also assigns an "s" to this letter but it was originally the sound for the 15th letter "sin".

† Tav

Pictographic (form): The Ancient picture † is a type of "mark", probably of two sticks crossed to mark a place similar to the Egyptian hieroglyph of ⊕, that is two crossed sticks.

Mnemonic (meaning): *Mark, Sign, Signature, Identification* -- as a marker to identify people, places or things; *Room, Desert, Dwelling* -- as marked

Syllabic (name): The Modern Hebrew, Arabic and Greek names for this letter is תו / tav (or taw), meaning, mark. This letter retains the original two-letter word.

Phonetic (sound): Hebrew, Greek and Arabic agree that the sound for this letter is "t".

Appendix B - Learn to Read Ancient Hebrew

Introduction

Learning to read the ancient Hebrew language is a fairly simple matter since our English alphabet and language are derived from the ancient Hebrew alphabet and language. For instance, the picture, name and sound of the Hebrew letter "Ⴁ", can easily be associated with the word "game". The picture is a foot, which is used to play games[46]. The sound for the letter is therefore "g". It is now an easy step to learning the original name of the letter, which is gam[47].

In addition, the pictograph of each letter is the origin for our own English alphabet. The similarities to the ancient Hebrew alphabet and ours will also assist in learning the letters. The letter "G"[48] originated in the Hebrew letter "Ⴁ".

Picture

The original pictographic script of "early Hebrew".

---

[46] The word "game" comes from the Latin "gamb", meaning "leg".
[47] The vowels in the names will be pronounced as follows; a = f<u>a</u>ther, e = gr<u>e</u>y, i = f<u>ee</u>t, o = b<u>o</u>ne, u = t<u>u</u>ne.
[48] The letter "G" was formed out of the letter "C".

English letter

Each Hebrew letter will be associated with the English letter that derived from it. By being able to see the English letter within the Hebrew, the sound of the letter will more easily be remembered. The English letter will be oriented to a form closer resemblance of the Hebrew letter.

English name

The name of the letter will be learned with an English word. Many times a word from one culture will be slightly changed when adopted by another culture. There are certain letters that are commonly exchanged for another as listed below.

Aspirates - s, sh, ts, x, z
Gutturals - g, c, ch, h, k, q
Lip letters - b, f, p, v, w
Tooth letters - d, t
Liquids - l, r
Nasals - m, n
Vowels - a, e, i, o, u

Hebrew name

The original Hebrew name of the letter will then be revealed. In most cases, the English word is very close to the Hebrew. The name of each letter is also the Hebrew word for what the picture is. For example, the letter "" is a picture of a door, the Hebrew name for this letter is "dal", which in Hebrew means, "door".

Hebrew sound

The sound of the letter will be defined and is always the sound of the first letter of the Hebrew name.

Hebrew meaning

The meaning of the letters will be explained. These meanings will be related to the picture and name.

Once the letters are understood in their original Hebrew context, we will look at a few Hebrew words, which are formed by combining letters together. The meanings of these letters will then supply the definition to the Hebrew word. The pronunciation of the word will also be seen through the letters of the word.

Picture: Head of an ox
The ox was the strongest and most versatile animal among the Hebrews livestock. The ox was used to pull carts or a plow, it provided meat and leather and it was one of the animals used in sacrifices.

English Letter: ∀ (A)

English Name: All
This animal was the "all" powerful and "all" versatile animal of the Hebrews.

Hebrew name: al
The original name is the same as the English equivalent. The Hebrew word "al" means "ox" and is the original name of this letter. This is the only Hebrew letter used as a vowel only. In Modern Hebrew this letter is silent.

Meaning: Strong
Because of the great strength of the ox.

Picture: Tent
The Hebrews lived in goat hair tents that were divided into two halves, male and female sections, and divided by a wall. The above picture is a representation of the floor plan to the tent. The entrance is seen at the top left.

English Letter: ⬜ **(B)**

English Name: Bed
The tent was the place where the family laid their "bed".

Hebrew name: Bet
The original name for this letter is bet meaning, tent or family in Hebrew. A common sound shift over time is a "t" sound to a "d" as they are both similar in sound and are formed by the tongue and teeth.

Hebrew sound: b, bh (v)
The "b" sound is a stop meaning; the sound is made and abruptly stops and is used at the beginning of a word. The "bh" is a spirant meaning; the sound can continue and is used when the letter is not at the beginning of the word.

Meaning: Family
The function of the tent is to provide a covering for the family. This letter can also mean "in" or "inside" as the family resides "in" the tent.

L

Picture: Foot

English Letter: G

English Name: Game
The Hebrews were always on their feet for traveling, working as well as playing "games".

Hebrew name: gam
Our word "Game" comes from the Latin word "gam" meaning "leg" coming from the Hebrew word "gam" meaning "foot".

Hebrew sound: g

Meaning: Gather
Men and animals would walk, on foot, gathering at the nearest watering hole. This letter can also mean walk or carry.

Picture: Door
A curtain suspended from a horizontal pole covered the entrance of the Hebrew's tent. The picture of this letter represents the "door" of the tent.

English Letter: ▽ **(D)**

English Name: Door

Hebrew name: dal
Another common shift in sounds is the "l" to an "r". The Hebrew word "dal" meaning "door" became our word "door".

Hebrew sound: d

Meaning: Hang
The door hangs down over the opening of the tent. This letter can also meant movement as one moves in and out of the tent through the door.

Picture: Man with arms raised
The picture is of a man with his arms outstretched at seeing a great sight.

English Letter: ⊔ (E)

English Name: Hey
A man waves to another and says "hey".

Hebrew name: hey
There is no change from the English equivalent to the original Hebrew. This is a picture of a man pointing at a wonderful sight and saying, "look". The Hebrew word "hey" means "behold", or "look".

Hebrew sound: h, e
This letter was used as both a consonant and a vowel.

Meaning: Look
The man pointing out a wonderful sight says, "look". This letter can also mean sigh or breath.

Picture: Peg
Ropes attached to pegs driven into the ground supported the tent. These pegs were made of a branched piece of hardwood preventing the ropes from slipping off the peg.

English Letter: F

English Name: Wave
No English word is derived from this letter but the picture is similar to the hand of a man "waving".

Hebrew name: waw
The Hebrew word for a peg is "waw".

Hebrew sound: w, o, u
This letter was used as both a consonant and a vowel.

Meaning: Secure
A peg is used to secure the tent in place. This letter can also mean add as a peg or nail can be used to add something to something else.

Picture: Mattock
The picture is of a mattock, an agricultural tool for working the fields of crops.

English Letter: Z

English Name: Z
There is no English word derived from this Hebrew letter but it is similar to the letter "Z" which did evolve out of this letter.

Hebrew name: zayin
The Hebrew word for Mattock is "zayin".

Hebrew sound: z

Meaning: Cut
The mattock is representative of tools used for cutting. As the mattock can be used as a weapon, this letter can mean a weapon. It can also mean food, which comes from the harvest.

Picture: Wall

English Letter: (H)

English Name: Half
The tent was divided into two sections, with a wall separating the tent in "half".

Hebrew name: chets
The Hebrew word "chets" means a "wall" as well as "half" as the wall divides the tent in half.

Hebrew sound: ch
The Hebrew sound, written as "ch", is not used in English. It is a hard guttural sound made in the back of the throat as in the German name "Bach" or the word "ich".

Meaning: Separate
The purpose of the wall is to separate the two halves of the tent. This letter can also mean outside as the walls of the tent separate the people inside from what is outside.

Picture: Basket
Baskets were common and used to store foods and supplies.

English Letter: No English letter is derived from this Hebrew letter.

English Name: Tote
A "tote" is a type of basket.

Hebrew name: Tet
The Hebrew word "tet" means "basket" and is the original name for this letter.

Hebrew sound: t

Meaning: Contain
A basket contains the foods and possessions of the family. This letter can also mean mud or clay as this material was often used to make baskets.

Picture: Hand
The picture is the hand and arm of a man.

English Letter: **(I)**

English Name: Yard
The length of the arm, from fingertip to elbow is called a cubit. Our word "yard", as a measurement, is the length of the arm.

Hebrew name: Yad
The Hebrew word "yad" means, "hand".

Hebrew sound: y, i
This letter was used as both a consonant and a vowel.

Meaning: Work
The hand is the part of the body that does the work. This letter can also mean throw or worship, both is actions of the hand.

Picture: Palm
The picture is the open palm of the hand.

English Letter: ☒ **(K)**

English Name: Cup
The palm facing up and bent forms a "cup" shape.

Hebrew name: Kaph
The Hebrew word for the palm of the hand is "Kaph".

Hebrew sound: k, kh
The Hebrew sound, written as "kh", is similar to the "ch" and is a hard guttural sound made in the back of the throat as in the German name "Bach" or the word "ich".
The "k" is a stop consonant, while the "kh" is a spirant.

Meaning: Bend
The palm is representative of anything that is bent. This letter can also mean open or allow, as opening an opportunity.

J

Picture: Shepherd staff
The Hebrews raised sheep for wool, food, leather and milk. The Hebrew shepherd always carried a staff that could be used as a weapon to protect the flock from predators as well as to discipline the sheep.

English Letter: ⌐ (L)

English Name: Lamb
The staff also had a curved end that could be used to pull a "lamb".

Hebrew name: lam
The Hebrew word for the shepherd staff is "lam".

Hebrew sound: l

Meaning: Authority
The staff is seen as the authority and protection of the shepherd over his flock. The kings' scepter comes from this imagery. This letter can also mean to or toward as the staff s used to guide the flock to a particular direction. It can also mean a yoke, which was a staff on the shoulders and also used to guide the ox in a particular direction.

ᴍᴍ

Picture: Water
The picture is of the waves of water on the sea.

English Letter: M

English Name: M
There is no English word derived from this letter, but our letter "M" was derived from this letter.

Hebrew name: mah
The Hebrew word for water is "mayim", a plural word, from the singular word "mah".

Hebrew sound: m

Meaning: Mighty
The Hebrews saw the sea as a mighty and chaotic place because of the storms and turbulent waters. This letter can also mean the red juice (water) of the grape or the red blood (water) of man.

Picture: Seed
The picture is a seed with the root coming out of it.

English Letter: И (N)

English Name: New
The seed is the beginning of "new" life.

Hebrew name: nun
The Hebrew word for a continuation of new life is "nun".

Hebrew sound: n

Meaning: Continue
The seed is the continuation of a new generation. This letter can also mean a son or heir as the next generation.

Picture: Thorn
The desert of the Hebrews has many species of thorns and thistles. The picture is a thorn that attaches itself to the flesh causing pain.

English Letter: X

English Name: Sin
Our word "sin" comes from this letter as it also causes pain in our flesh like a thorn.

Hebrew name: sin
The Hebrew word for a thorn is "sin".

Hebrew sound: s

Meaning: Hold
A thorn holds onto the skin or fur of animals. This letter can also mean to protect. When a shepherd was in the wilderness overnight with the flock, he would construct a corral of thorn bushes to protect the flock from predators.

Picture: Eye

English Letter: O
When the Greeks adopted the Hebrew alephbet, this letter became the omicron, a vowel becoming the "O" in our alphabet.

English Name: Eye

Hebrew name: ghayin
The Hebrew word for "eye" is "ghayin" often pronounced as "ayin", the origin of our word "eye".

Hebrew sound: gh
The "gh" sound is like the "ng" in "ring". The sound is soft and often silent.

Meaning: See
The eye is for seeing. This letter can also mean know as we know our surroundings through the eye.

Picture: Mouth
The picture is the mouth and represents something that is open.

English Letter: ⊐ (P)

English Name: Pit
There is no English word from this letter but can represent a "pit" as it is an open hole.

Hebrew name: pey
The Hebrew word for "mouth" is "pey".

Hebrew sound: p, ph
The "P" is a stop consonant while the "ph" is a spirant.

Meaning: Open
The mouth is the opening into the body. This letter can also mean edge, as the mouth is the edge of the opening.

Picture: Man lying on his side

English Letter: No English letter is derived from this Hebrew letter.

English Name: Side

Hebrew name: tsad
The Hebrew word "tsad" is the origin of our word "side".

Hebrew sound: ts
The original sound for this letter is a "ts" as in our word "pot<u>s</u>".

Meaning: Side
One lies down on his side. This letter can also mean to lie in wait or to hunt by lying in wait for the prey.

Picture: Sun at the horizon
This is a picture of the sun at the horizon where the light is concentrated at this point, while the rest of the sky is dark.

English Letter: ☉ (Q)

English Name: Come
The "coming" together of the light.

Hebrew name: quph
The Hebrew name for this letter is "quph" meaning the circling of the sun around the earth.

Hebrew sound: q

Meaning: Condense
When the sun is at the horizon the light is condensed at the horizon. This letter can also mean to circle.

Picture: Head of a man

English Letter: ᴙ **(R)**

English Name: Raise
The picture is the head of a man that is "raised" up to look.

Hebrew name: resh
The Hebrew word for the head is "resh", the origin of our word "raise".

Hebrew sound: r

Meaning: Top
The head, as the top of the body is representative of anything that is at the top, head or beginning of something. This letter can also mean first as the top in rank or beginning as the top of a time.

ШЦ

Picture: Teeth
The picture is of the two front teeth.

English Letter: Ꮿ **(S)**

English Name: Shine
The whiteness of the teeth "shine".

Hebrew name: Shin
The Hebrew word for "tooth" is "shin".

Hebrew sound: sh

Meaning: Sharp
The front teeth are sharp for cutting meat. As the teeth are used to press down on the food, this letter can also mean press, eat or devour.

Picture: Mark
The picture is of two crossed sticks as a mark to identify a location.

English Letter: T

English Name: Target
A mark such as a "target" one aims at when shooting.

Hebrew name: taw
The Hebrew word for a mark is "taw".

Hebrew sound: t

Meaning: Sign
A mark is used as a sign to identify someone or something.

Appendix B – Learn Ancient Hebrew

Letter	Picture	Name	Sound	English Derivitives	
⅄	Ox	Al	a	All	A
⌶	Tent	Bet	b	Bed	B
⌐	Foot	Gam	g	Game	C
⊓	Door	Dal	d	Door	D
⌁	Arms	Hey	h,e	Hi	E
Y	Peg	Waw	w,o,u	-	F
⊏	Mattock	Zan	z	-	Z
⊞	Wall	Hhets	hh	Half	H
⊗	Basket	Thet	th	Tote	-
⊐	Hand	Yad	y,i	Yard	I
⨆	Palm	Kaph	k	Cup	K
∪	Staff	Lam	l	Lamb	L
⁓	Water	Mah	m	-	M
↘	Seed	Nun	n	New	N
⩬	Thorn	Sin	s	Sin	X
⊘	Eye	Ghan	gh	Eye	O
⊃	Mouth	Pey	p	Pit	P
⌒	Side	Tsad	ts	Side	-
⊸	Horizon	Quph	q	-	Q
⅁	Head	Resh	r	Raise	R
⊔	Teeth	Shin	sh	Shine	S
†	Mark	Taw	t	-	T

Appendix C - *History of the Hebrew Script*

The following are twenty-four tables (two for each letter) documenting the history of each letter. The first table for each letter lists all the various forms of the letter as found in ancient documents and inscriptions portraying the 2,000 year evolution of each letter through its journeys from one culture to the next.

Since one of the primary purposes of this book is to assist the student of Hebrew with learning the ancient Hebrew language and alphabet, the second table is the evolution of each letter from its original pictograph to five modern alphabets. The evolution of each letter will enable the student to more easily recognize the ancient letters by their association with English as well as modern Hebrew, Greek, Arabic and Samaritan (for those familiar with these alphabets).

Appendix C – History of the Hebrew Script

⅄ - Al

	2,000	1,500	1,000	500	100
Canaanite	⅄ ⅄	ᛕ ⅄ ᛕ	⅄		
Hebrew		⅄	⅊	⅊	F
Phonecian		ᛕ ⅄ ᛕ	⅊	⅊ ⅊	
Aramaic			⅊ ⅊	⅄ ⅄	⅄
Greek			⅁ ∀ ∧ ⅄	△ A	A
S. Arabian			ⴼ ⴼ ⴼ		
Punic				✕	
Latin					A
Samaritan					ⴹ
Arabic					∖

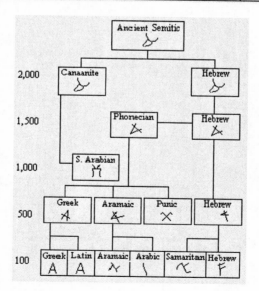

Ancient Hebrew Language and Alphabet

⊔⊐ / Bet

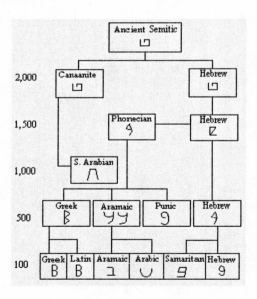

	2,000	1,500	1,000	500	100
Canaanite	⊔⊐⊔⊐	◁▽Ɀ	𝟿𝟫		
Hebrew		𝟫	𝟫𝟫	𝟜	𝟫
Phonecian		𝟥	𝟫𝟫𝟫	𝟦𝟫𝟫	
Aramaic			𝟫𝟫	𝖸𝖹	⊐
Greek			𝟤𝟪𝟥𝟤	ßB	B
S. Arabian			∧		
Punic				𝟫	
Latin					B
Samaritan					𝟫
Arabic					∪

94

⌐ / Gam

	2,000	1,500	1,000	500	100
Canaanite	⌐ ∟	∧ > Γ ∧	∧ ∧ ⟩		
Hebrew		ℸℸ	ℸ ∖	∖	ℸ
Phonecian		⟩ ⟩	∖		
Aramaic			ℸ	∧ λ	ℷ
Greek			⟩ ⟩ ∧ ℸ	Γ Γ	Γ
S. Arabian			ℸ ℿ		
Punic				λ ∧	
Latin					C G
Samaritan					ℸ
Arabic					≻

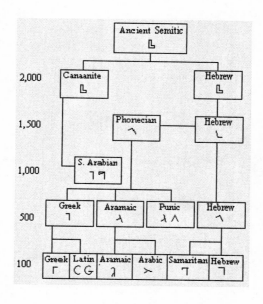

⊔ / Dal

	2,000	1,500	1,000	500	100
Canaanite	⊔ ▷	▽ ◁	◁		
Hebrew			Δ ◁	Δ	◁
Phonecian			٩ ▷ ٩		
Aramaic			△	Ч Ч	┐
Greek			Δ	△ ▷ Ð	△
S. Arabian			ꓷ		
Punic	·			٩	
Latin					Ð
Samaritan					ꟼ
Arabic					ﯼ

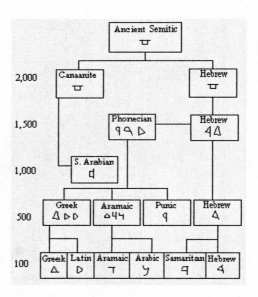

⟨ / Hey

	2,000	1,500	1,000	500	100
Canaanite	⟨ ⟨	⟨⟨⟨⟨	⟨ ⟨ ⟨		
Hebrew		⟨	⟨⟨	⟨	⟨
Phonecian		⟨ ⟨	⟨⟨	⟨⟨⟨	
Aramaic		⟨	⟨ ⟨	⟨⟨⟨⟨	⟨
Greek			⟨⟨	⟨E	E
S. Arabian			⟨ ⟨		
Punic				⟨	
Latin					E
Samaritan					⟨
Arabic					⟨

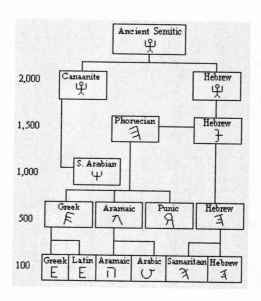

97

Y / Waw

	2,000	1,500	1,000	500	100
Canaanite	Y⅄ꟼ	Yꟼ	٦		
Hebrew		Y	ৎ F	ৎ	ৎ
Phonecian		Y	५५	५५	
Aramaic			YYY	٦	٦
Greek			ㄱㄱ	FF	Υ
S. Arabian			Ⓘ		
Punic				५	
Latin					F
Samaritan					⋋
Arabic					٩

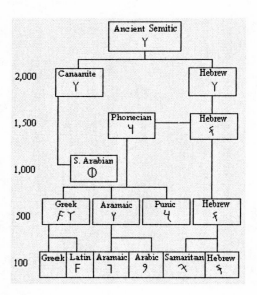

98

ᴛ / Zan

	2,000	1,500	1,000	500	100
Canaanite	[glyphs]	[glyphs]	[glyphs]		
Hebrew		[glyph]	[glyphs]	[glyph]	[glyph]
Phonecian		[glyphs]	[glyph]	[glyphs]	
Aramaic			[glyph]	[glyphs]	[glyph]
Greek			[glyphs]	[glyph]	[glyph]
S. Arabian			[glyphs]		
Punic				[glyph]	
Latin					[glyph]
Samaritan					[glyph]
Arabic					[glyph]

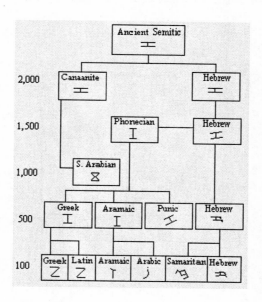

ⲙ / Hhets

	2,000	1,500	1,000	500	100
Canaanite	𒀀 𒀀	𒀀 ⲙ 目	目 目 H		
Hebrew		目	目 目	目	目
Phonecian		目 目	目 目	ⲃ	
Aramaic			目 ⲏ	ⲏⲏ	ⲡ
Greek			H目目目	目H	H
S. Arabian			Ψ		
Punic				目	
Latin					H
Samaritan					目
Arabic					7

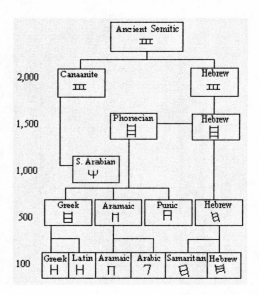

⊗ / Thet

	2,000	1,500	1,000	500	100
Canaanite	○→	⊗ ⊕	⊕		
Hebrew		⊗ ⊕	⊗ ⊕	ʊ	♡
Phonecian		⊗ ⊕	⊕ ⊌	⊌	
Aramaic		⊕ ⊗		6 6 6	ʊ
Greek			⊗ ⊕ ⊖	⊖	⊖
S. Arabian			▯▯		
Punic				⊌	
Latin					
Samaritan					⊲
Arabic					b

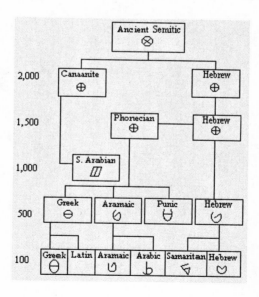

Ancient Hebrew Language and Alphabet

⊐ / Yad

	2,000	1,500	1,000	500	100
Canaanite	⅀⌇ ⌇	⌇⌐⌇	ⱫⱫ		
Hebrew		Ⱬ	Ⱬ⌐	Ⱬ	Ⱬ
Phonecian		ⱫⱫⱫ	Ⱬ⌐∼	Ⱬ∿∿	
Aramaic			ⱫⱫⱫ	⋋⋋⋌⌐	⌐
Greek			123242	1	I
S. Arabian			℗		
Punic				2⌐2	
Latin					I
Samaritan					⌐y
Arabic					S

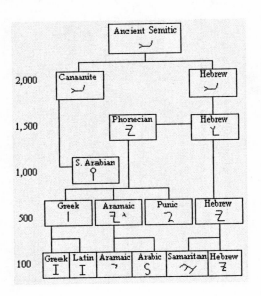

⨑ / Kaph

	2,000	1,500	1,000	500	100
Canaanite	☁ ᴟ ᴟ	ᴠ ᴠ Y	ϤϤϤϤ		
Hebrew		ᴠ	ϤϤϤϤ	ϟ	𝔂
Phonecian		ᴠ	ϤϤϤ	ϤϤ	
Aramaic			Y	ϤϤϟ	⊤Ɔ
Greek			ϪK	K	K
S. Arabian		⌐			
Punic				ϟϟ	
Latin					K
Samaritan					𝔂
Arabic					⌡

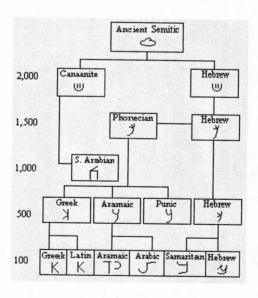

103

ل / Lam

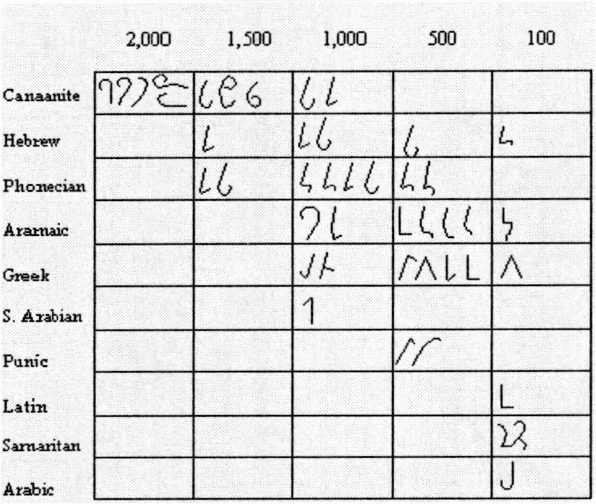

	2,000	1,500	1,000	500	100
Canaanite	ꝁꝁⵒ⳽	ƐƐ6	ll		
Hebrew		l	ll	l	Ь
Phonecian		ll	ʟʟʟʟ	ʟʟ	
Aramaic			ꝃl	ʟʟᏟᏟ	ﬥ
Greek			Jʟ	⋀Ꮮʟʟ	⋀
S. Arabian			1		
Punic				//	
Latin					L
Samaritan					ꝰᏃ
Arabic					�J

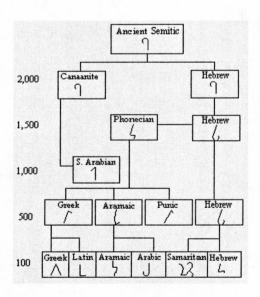

ᴧᴧ / Mem

	2,000	1,500	1,000	500	100
Canaanite	ᴧᴧ ᴧᴧ ᴧᴧ ᴧᴧ	⌇⌇ ⌇⌇ ⌇	५५		
Hebrew		⌇	५ᴍᴍ	५	५
Phonecian		⌇	५५५ ⌇	५५	
Aramaic		⌇⌇	५५	५५	ᗞᗞ
Greek			ᴍᴍ	ᴍᴍ	ᴍ
S. Arabian			⌇		
Punic				⌇ ✕	
Latin					ᴍ
Samaritan					५
Arabic					⟋ᴑ

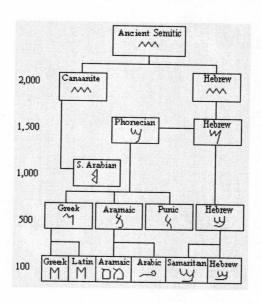

⸜ / Nun

	2,000	1,500	1,000	500	100
Canaanite	⸜⸜⸜	ʮʮʮ⸗	ʮʮʮ		
Hebrew			ʮʮʮ	ч	ч
Phonecian		ʮʮʮ	ʮʮʮʮʮ	ʮ	
Aramaic		ʮʮ	ʮ1	ʮʮʮʮʮ	1ᴶ
Greek			ʮʮN	Nʮʮ	N
S. Arabian			ʮʮ		
Punic				1ſ	
Latin					N
Samaritan					ʒʒ
Arabic					Ỏ

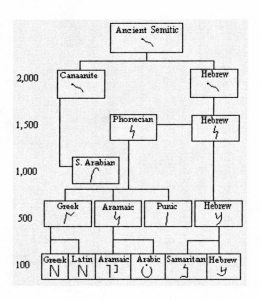

彡 / Sin

	2,000	1,500	1,000	500	100
Canaanite	(glyphs)	(glyphs)	(glyphs)		
Hebrew		(glyph)	(glyphs)	(glyph)	
Phonecian		(glyphs)	(glyphs)	(glyph)	
Aramaic		(glyphs)	(glyphs)	(glyphs)	(glyph)
Greek			(glyphs)	(glyphs)	(glyph)
S. Arabian			(glyph)		
Punic				(glyph)	
Latin					×
Samaritan					(glyph)
Arabic					

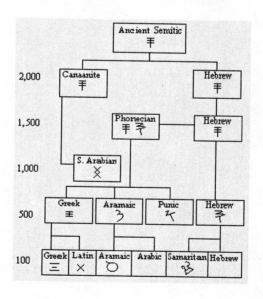

◉ / Ghan

	2,000	1,500	1,000	500	100
Canaanite	◉()◉ ◯()◉	○ ⊙	○		
Hebrew		○	○ ◊	○	▽
Phonecian		○ C	○ ∪ ◌	○ ∪	
Aramaic			⊙	∪ ∨ У	≫
Greek			○	○	○
S. Arabian			○		
Punic				○	
Latin					○
Samaritan					▽
Arabic					Ч

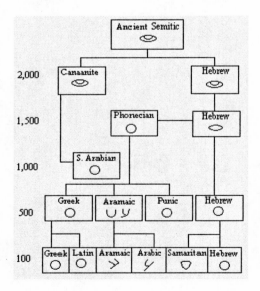

◯ / Pey

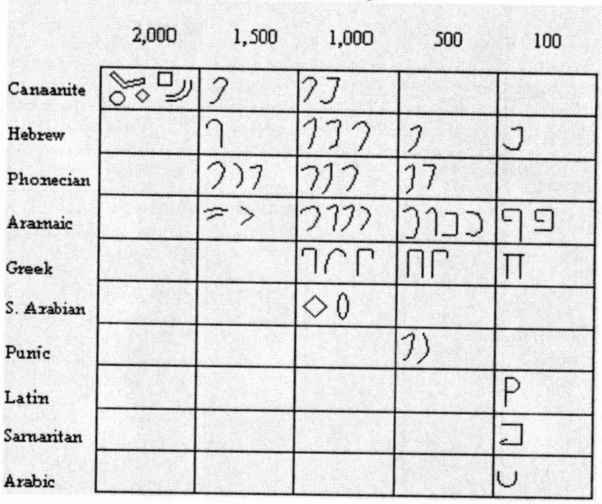

	2,000	1,500	1,000	500	100
Canaanite	◯ ◇ ⍫	フ	フ⅃		
Hebrew		�)	フフ フ	フ	⅃
Phonecian		)フフ	フフフ	フフ	
Aramaic		≂ >	フフフフ	フフ⅃⅃	フ ⅁
Greek			⌐⌐⌐	⊓⌐	⊓
S. Arabian			◇ 0		
Punic				フ)	
Latin					P
Samaritan					⅃
Arabic					∪

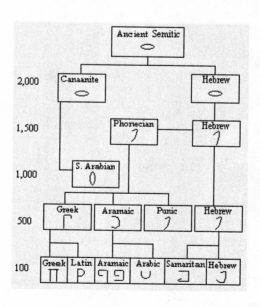

109

Ancient Hebrew Language and Alphabet

᧏ / Tsad

	2,000	1,500	1,000	500	100
Canaanite	ⵟⵟⵟⵟ	ⵟⵟ	ⵣⵣ		
Hebrew		ⵟ	ⵟⵟ	ⵟ	
Phonecian		ⵟⵟⵟ	ⵟⵟ	ⵟⵟ	
Aramaic		ⵟ	ⵟⵟ	ⵟⵟⵟⵟ	ⵟⵟ
Greek			M	M	
S. Arabian			ⵟⵟ		
Punic				ⵟⵟ	
Latin					
Samaritan					ⵟⵟ
Arabic					ⵜ

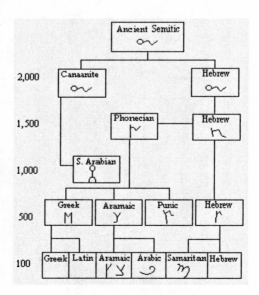

Appendix C – History of the Hebrew Script

⊖ / Quph

	2,000	1,500	1,000	500	100
Canaanite	⌀⊖⌀ ϙ ϙ		ϙ		
Hebrew		ϙ	ψϘ	φ	ψ
Phonecian		ϙ	ϘϘϘϘ	ϘϘϘ	
Aramaic		ϙ ϙ	ϤϤϙ	ϘϘϞ	ϙ
Greek			ϙϙ		
S. Arabian			ϙ		
Punic				ϙϙ	
Latin					Q
Samaritan					▽ϙ
Arabic					؟

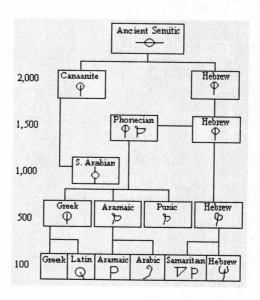

111

ᴿ / Resh

	2,000	1,500	1,000	500	100
Canaanite	የ૬?የ૬ףዋ		ዋ		
Hebrew		ዋ	499	ዋ	ዋ
Phonecian		ዋ	9499	99	
Aramaic		99	Ч	4ግግ	ገ
Greek			999	₽₽₽	₽
S. Arabian			)		
Punic				ዋ	
Latin					R
Samaritan					99
Arabic					)

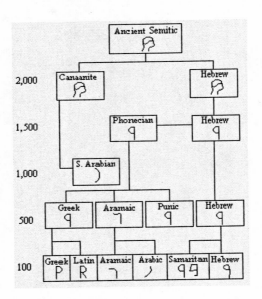

⊔⊔ / Shin

	2,000	1,500	1,000	500	100
Canaanite					
Hebrew					
Phonecian					
Aramaic					
Greek					
S. Arabian					
Punic					
Latin					
Samaritan					
Arabic					

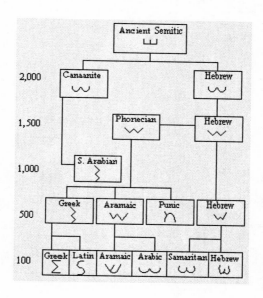

113

Ancient Hebrew Language and Alphabet

† / Taw

	2,000	1,500	1,000	500	100
Canaanite	† +	✕	† ✕		
Hebrew		+	✕ ㆠ✕	✕	✕
Phonecian		✕ +	✕+ㆠㆠ	ㆠㆠ	
Aramaic		✕ +	ㆠㆠ	ㆠㆠ	ㆠ
Greek			†TT		T
S. Arabian			✕		
Punic				ㆠㆠ	
Latin					T
Samaritan					ㆠㆠ
Arabic					ᴗ

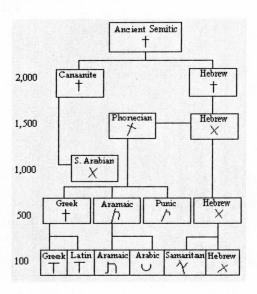

Appendix D – Alphabet Charts

Ancient Hebrew

Script	Picture	Meaning	Name	/Sound
𐤀	Head of an ox	strong, power, leader	al	a
𐤁	Tent floorplan	family, house, in	bet	b,bh
𐤂	Foot	gather, walk, carry	gam	g
𐤃	Tent door	move, hang, enter	dal	d
𐤄	Arms raised	look, reveal, sigh	hey	h,e
𐤅	Tent peg	add, secure, hook	waw	w,o,u
𐤆	Mattock	food, cut, weapon	zan	z
𐤇	Tent wall	outside, divide, half	hhets	hh
⊗	Clay basket	surround, contain, mud	thet	th
𐤉	Closed hand	work, throw, worship	yad	y,i
𐤊	Open palm	bend, allow, tame	kaph	k,kh
𐤋	Shepherd staff	teach, yoke, to, bind	lam	l
𐤌	Water	chaos, mighty, blood	mah	m
𐤍	Sprouting seed	continue, heir, son	nun	n
𐤎	Thorn	grab, hate, protect	sin	s
𐤏	Eye	watch, know, shade	ghan	gh
𐤐	Open mouth	blow, scatter, edge	pey	p,ph
𐤑	Man on his side	wait, chase, hunt	tsad	ts
𐤒	Horizon	condense, circle, time	quph	q
𐤓	Head of a man	first, beginning, top	resh	r
𐤔	Two front teeth	sharp, press, eat, two	shin	sh
†	Crossed sticks	mark, sign, signature	taw	t

Modern Hebrew

Script	Name	Sound	Derivatives Greek	Latin
א	aleph	silent	A	A
ב	beyt	b,bh	B	B
ג	gimel	g	Γ	C,G
ד	dalet	d	Δ	D
ה	hey	h	E	E
ו	vav	v,o,u	Υ*	F
ז	zayin	z	Z	Z
ח	hhet	hh	H	H
ט	tet	t	Θ	-
י	yud	y	I	I,J
כ,ך	kaph	k,kh	K	K
ל	lamed	l	Λ	L
מ,ם	Mem	m	M	M
נ,ן	nun	n	N	N
ס	samech	s	Ξ	X
ע	ayin	silent	O	O
פ,ף	pey	ph	Π	P
צ,ץ	tsadey	ts	M*	-
ק	quph	q	Q*	Q
ר	resh	r	P	R
ש,שׂ	shin,sin	sh,s	Σ	S
ת	tav	t	T	T

* Ancient letter not carried over into Modern Greek.

Appendix E - Ancient Hebrew Parent Root Dictionary

Purpose of the Lexicon

All Modern Hebrew dictionaries and lexicons are written from a Western/Greek perspective, ignoring the original Hebraic concrete understanding of words. This dictionary is written to fill this hole of Biblical understanding. The goal of the dictionary is to show the original understanding of Biblical words based on the Hebrew culture and thought so that the Modern reader can see the text through the eyes of the Ancient Hebrews who wrote it. This dictionary will only include the parent roots, which lay the foundation for all the child roots, and words that are derived from it. A more comprehensive dictionary including the child roots and words will be completed in the future.

Cross reference to Strong's numbers

To find the parent root of a given Hebrew word, find the Strong's number using any exhaustive concordance keyed to Strong's. Appendix E will list the Strong's number[49] followed by the Ancient Hebrew parent root number. The

---

[49] Only those words which are derived from a parent or child root will be listed

117

definition of the parent root will then provide the concrete understanding to this word.

Appendix E will also list the Ancient Hebrew parent root number followed by the Strong's numbers of all the words derived from the parent. This will allow the student to see all the words that are related to each other from the parent.

How to use the Lexicon

Below is a Sample entry from the lexicon describing the format of the parent root entry.

008[1] 𐤌𐤏[2] AHh[3] strong   wall[4]   -- Hearth[5]: The hearth around the fire protected the house from the heat and embers of the fire. The brothers of the house are the protectors by surrounding the house to protect it.[6]

~~~~~~~~~~~~~~~~~~~~~~~~~~~~~~~~~~

1. The parent root number. This number is derived alphabetically. For example, the word 𐤏𐤏 is 001, 𐤌𐤏 is 002, 𐤋𐤏 is 003, etc. Some numbers will be missing, such as "001" as there is no Hebrew word in the Bible derived from this parent root.
2. The pictographic Hebrew for the parent root.
3. A transliteration of the Hebrew letters into Roman letters.
4. The meaning of the Hebrew pictographs of the parent root. This definition is based on the meanings of the two letters of the root. The letter 𐤏 is an ox meaning

118

strong, and the **L** is a wall, with a combined definition of "strong wall".

5. An English word equivalent to the Hebrew meaning of the parent root. The concrete understanding of a strong wall is a "hearth".

6. The cultural background and meaning of the Hebrew parent root. All of the child roots and words derived from the parent will be related in meaning.

Following the Parent Root Lexicon is a cross-reference table (Appendix F) for the Ancient Hebrew Lexicon and Strong's Dictionary. By looking up the Strong's number in the Appendix you can find the Parent Root that this word is derived from. By looking up the Parent Root number you can find all of the Hebrew words, by Strong's number, derived from this root.

002 ⌐◝ᐯ   **ABh**   **strength of the house -- Pole:** The poles provided the strength, support and structure of the tent. The pole is pointed at one end so that it can be thrust into the ground and can double as a weapon against an enemy. The father of the family also provides the strength, support and structure to the household. The father fulfilled many functions for the family. He was the commander of the family army, provider of offspring to continue the family line, the priest and teacher. A desire is what one stands in support of.

~~~~~~~~~~~~~~~~~~~~~~~~~~~~~~~

004 ⊓◝ᐯ   **AD**   **strength at the tent door --
Smoke:** The cooking fires of the family were located at the tent door. A large amount of smoke could accumulate at the door causing discomfort to the family. A fire poker is used to turn, arrange and gather the wood in the fire to reduce the smoke. A thought is a turning over and bringing together.

~~~~~~~~~~~~~~~~~~~~~~~~~~~~~~~

005 ⚤◝ᐯ   **AH**   **strong breath -- Sigh:** The ox snorts (sighs) when desiring food. The sigh of one searching for; a person (who), place (where), thing (what), time (when) or event (how).

~~~~~~~~~~~~~~~~~~~~~~~~~~~~~~~

007 ⌐◝ᐯ   **AZ**   **strong harvest -- Time:** The farmers year revolved around the harvest. The times of the harvests were at specific times according to the solar calendar.

008 〰〴 **AHh** **strong wall -- Hearth:** The hearth around the fire protected the house from the heat and embers of the fire. The brothers of the house are the protectors by surrounding the house to protect it.

009 ⊗〴 **ATh** **ox contained -- Tame:** The ox, as the strongest of the livestock, needed to be corralled so that it may be tamed in order to be trained to do work.

012 ᴊ〴 **AL** **ox in a yoke -- Muscle:** Oxen, the strongest of the livestock, were placed in a yoke (see Isaiah 9:4) in order to harness their power for pulling loads such as a wagon or plow. Often two oxen were yoked together. An older, more experienced ox would be teamed up (yoked) with a younger, less experienced ox. The pictographs of this parent root can also be interpreted as a "strong authority" where the ox represents strength and the staff of the shepherd represents his authority over the flock. The older ox in the yoke is the "strong authority" who, through the yoke, teaches the younger ox. The yoking together of two parties. A treaty or covenant binds two parties together through an oath (yoke). The oath included blessings for abiding by the covenant and curses for breaking the covenant (see Deuteronomy 28). The God of the Hebrews was seen as the older ox who is yoked to his people in a covenant relationship.

013 ᴍᵖ **AM**　**strong liquid -- Glue:** Glue was made by placing the hides of animals in a pot of boiling water. As the hide boiled, a thick sticky substance formed at the surface of the water. This substance was removed and used as a binding agent. The arm is seen as a glue as it encircles and holds together (a cubit was the length of the arm from elbow to fingertip). The mother of the family is the one who binds the family together by holding in her arms and by the work of her arms. The tribe is the larger family bound together by blood relation.

014 ᵥᵖ **AN**　**ox seed -- Produce:** The male searches out the female and approaches her for reproducing (see Jeremiah 2:24). A search for someone in order to produce something. A ship searches through the sea for a distant coastline (of an island or mainland) in search of the produce for trade. The fig tree produces fruit that is desirable and prolific, since the fig is green and blends in with the leaves, the fruit must be searched out. The searching may result in success or failure.

017 ⊃ᵖ **APh**　**ox mouth -- Nose:** The nostrils of the ox flare when snorting just as a man's does when he breaths heavy through the nose when in passion or anger. The heat of passion or cooking.

018 ᵃᵥᵖ **ATs**　**ox side -- Press:** An ox will often lean or press on something such as a fence, tree, or person causing it to move.

019 -●-𝄐 **AQ**   **? -- Wild goat**

020 𝄐 **AR**   **strong beginning -- Light:** The day (light) begins with the rising of the sun in the east. Additionally, the first day of creation (as a strong beginning) was the creation of light. The light brings order. Boxes are used for storing items to put them in order.

021 ⊔𝄐 **ASh**   **strong pressing -- Fire:** A fire is made by firmly pressing a wooden rod down onto a wooden board and spinning the rod with a bow drill. Wood dust is generated from the two woods rubbing together and is heated by the friction creating a small ember in the dust. Small tinder is then placed on the ember and is blown ignited the tinder. The pressing down of the soil to form a firm and flat surface. The pressing together of soil by God to form man (Genesis 2.7).

022 †𝄐 **AT**   **ox to the mark -- Plow:** The plow point is used to cut a deep furrow in the ground for planting seeds. When plowing a field with oxen, the plowman drives the oxen toward a distant mark in order to keep the furrow straight. A traveler arrives at his destination by following a mark. The traveling toward a mark, destination or person. The arrival of one to the mark. A "you" is an individual who has arrived to a "me". The coming toward a mark. A standard, or flag, with the family mark hangs as a sign. An agreement or covenant by two where a sign or mark of the agreement is made as a reminder to both parties.

~~~~~~~~~~~~~

024 ⌸⌸ **BBh** **great inside -- Pupil:** The eye is the window into the soul.

~~~~~~~~~~~~~

026 ⌸⌸ **BD** **tent door -- Separate:** The father of the tent often sat alone at the door of the tent. Here he could receive shade from the sun, watch over his household and watch the road for approaching strangers. Many things are separated from the whole. A branch is separated from the tree. A thread is separated from the cloth. A liar is separated from the family or causes a separation in the family because of his false words. A wanderer is one alone or lost. A place separated from people is a place of ruin. A liar is separated from the family or causes a separation in the family because of his false words.

~~~~~~~~~~~~~

027 ⌸⌸ **BH** **inside revealed -- Empty:** A space that is empty that needs to be filled. To come or go into a space is to fill it. A void within oneself that desires to be filled. A box.

~~~~~~~~~~~~~

029 ⌐ᒪ **BZ** **house harvested -- Plunder:** An enemy would plunder a household for goods to supply the troops. Disrespect and scorn are a plunder of the heart.

~~~~~~~~~~~~~~~~~~~~~

030 ᒲᒧ **BHh** **inside outside -- Slaughter:** A slaughter by the knife or sword where the inside is opened.

~~~~~~~~~~~~~~~~~~~~~

031 ⊗ᒧ **BTh** **house surrounded -- Refuge:** The home as a refuge. The home is the place for safe idle talk with the family.

~~~~~~~~~~~~~~~~~~~~~

033 Ⱳᒧ **BK** **? -- Tears:** Tears from a lamenting or billowing smoke in the eyes.

~~~~~~~~~~~~~~~~~~~~~

034 ↙ᒧ **BL** **? -- Flow:** A flowing or mixing of a liquid. A flowing of tears. An emptying by a flowing out or away. Vain as a useless flowing of work. Panic as a flowing of the insides. A flowing away of life and strength. A large flowing of water such as a flood, as the river rises and overflows its banks, the surrounding lands are flooded depositing the water for growing the crops

~~~~~~~~~~~~~~~~~~~~~

035 ∿ᒧ **BM** **? -- High:** Anything that is tall or high.

125

036 ‎בֹל‎ **BN** **house continues -- Tent panel:**
The tent was constructed of woven goat hair. Over time
the sun bleaches and weakens the goat hair necessitating
their continual replacement. Each year a new panel,
approximately 3' wide and the length of the tent, is made
by the women. The old panel is removed (being recycled
into a wall or floor) and the new strip is added to the tent.
Since the tent is only replaced one small piece at a time
the tent lasts forever. There are many similarities between
building a tent out of goat hair panels and the building of
a house out of sons (The idea of building a house with
sons can be seen in Genesis 30.3). Just as the tent panels
are added to continue the tent, sons are born to the family
to continue the family line. Just as the tent is continually
being renewed with new panels, the family is continually
being renewed with new sons. When building more
permanent structures, the hair strips are replaced with
stones as the major building material. Man-made stones
were made by mixing clay and straw to form bricks. The
tent was usually divided into two parts, one for the
females and the other for the male. The wall makes a
distinction between the two sides. The thumb as the part
of the body understood as the builder by the Hebrews.
The planning and building of a house, structure or family.

037 ‎בֹס‎ **BS** **house of thorn -- Corral:** A pen
constructed of thorn bushes to hold the livestock inside.
The ground inside is heavily trampled by the livestock.

038 ◎◻ **BGh** ? -- **Swell:** A gushing over or swelling up as an eruption or a fountain. An overwhelming desire.

040 ◦◻ **BTs** **in the side -- White Clay:** On the sides of the swamps and marshes, a white clay is gathered. The white clay was desirable for making pottery.

041 ◦◻ **BQ** ? -- **Bottle:** A container for storing and pouring out a liquid. A lesion that pours out liquid.

042 ◻ **BR** **house of heads -- Grain:** The plant family of grains such as wheat and barley have a cluster of seeds at the top of the stalk called "heads". These grains were used for food for both man and livestock. Livestock are fattened on grain to prepare them for the slaughter. The stalks of the grains were burned to make potash for making soap. What is cleaned with soap becomes white or bright. The fowl, fed on grain, becomes strong for the long flight. A "covenant" involves the cutting of a fat animal prepared for slaughter.

043 ⊔⊔ᗡ   **BSh**   **? -- Wither:** A drying up of a land, stream, plant, etc. Shame is one who has failed or dried up. The smell of a dried up marsh.

---

044 ✝ᗡ   **BT**   **tent mark -- House:** A family takes the name of the father or ancestral father which the family is descended from. This name becomes the mark of the family such as 'the house of Israel'. The house, tent or family.

---

046 ᗡᏉ   **GBh**   **lift the inside -- Dig:** Digging is performed by the work of the bent back. Wells, pits and cisterns are dug inside the ground and the dirt is lifted out. A locust with a long back that cuts leaves

---

047 ᏉᏉ   **GG**   **great lifting -- Roof:** The wall and roof of the tent are one piece of cloth that is lifted up onto the poles, which support it.

---

048 ⊓Ꮑ   **GD**   **gather the door -- Slit:** When one enters the tent, the door is opened by parting the door, making a slit for passing through. An attacker slices through the ranks making an opening for them to enter in. Any cut or furrow made for making an entrance. A troop or band of people. The water rushing by the riverbank undercuts a furrow inside the bank. The animal's tendon is used for making bowstrings and cords. The tendon is removed by making a slit in the flesh and entering for its removal.

~~~~~~~~~~~~~~~~~~~~~~

049 ⚥L GH lifter reveals -- Back: The back is used for lifting. A valley is surrounded by hills as the back of the landscape. Pride is the lifting up of ones self. A healing as a lifting of an illness.

~~~~~~~~~~~~~~~~~~~~~~

051 ⌐L GZ lift the harvest -- Sheer: The sheering and removal of the wool fleece from the sheep. The cutting or sheering of grass. A stump as a tree sheared. The back and forth sweeping action of a sickle cutting grasses.

~~~~~~~~~~~~~~~~~~~~~~

052 ⊓L GHh lift the wall -- Belly: when crawling into the tent, other than through the front entrance, one much lift the wall and slide in on the belly like a snake.

~~~~~~~~~~~~~~~~~~~~~~

056 ⌣L GL ? -- Round: Something that is round or a second coming around of a time or event. A pond as a round pool of water. Redemption is the buying back of someone or something. A dancing in a circle.

~~~~~~~~~~~~~~~~~~~~~~

057 〰️L **GM** **walking to water -- Gather:** The watering well or other place of water is a gathering place for drinking of men, animals and plants. Men and animals may walk great distances for these watering holes while plants grow in abundance in them. Any gathering of people, things or ideas. The reeds of the watering holes were made into ropes.

058 〽️L **GN** **gathering of seeds -- Garden:** A garden is a place for growing crops and is surrounded by a rock wall or hedge to protect it from grazing animals. A bowl as a container enclosed by walls.

060 ⊙L **GGh** **lifting the eye -- Gasp:** When taking a difficult breath such as in gasping or in death, the eyes roll up.

061 ⊂L **GPh** **? -- Close**

064 ℞L **GR** **walking man -- Traveler:** One traveling through his non-native land is a stranger to the people and culture. Because of the unknown territory, bandits and wild animals, he is often in fear. The native is responsible for providing and protecting the stranger according to Ancient custom. The throat is the place where fear is felt. When a stranger meets another he lays prostrate in homage to the other. Anger is the result of fear.

~~~~~~~~~~

065 ⊔⊔⊔ **GSh** **? -- Grope**

~~~~~~~~~~

066 ✝⊔ **GT** **foot marked -- Winepress:** After the grapes are placed in the wine vat, treaders walk in the vat to crush the grapes freeing up the juices. The treaders feet and lower parts of their clothing are stained red, a sign of their occupation (see Is 63:1-3).

~~~~~~~~~~

068 ⊔⊔ **DBh** **door of the tent -- Rest:** The door of the tent was the place of relaxation for the father. Here he would watch his family, livestock and the road for approaching visitors (see Genesis 18:1). A relaxing in a quiet place. A slow walk due to a sorrow or loss.

~~~~~~~~~~

069 ⊔⊔ **DG** **moving foot -- Fish:** The tail of a fish moves back and forth to propel itself through the water. The back and forth movement of the fish's tail. A net full of fish is an abundance or increase. A net as a tool for catching fish.

~~~~~~~~~~

070 ⊔⊔ **DD** **two danglers -- Breasts:** The part of the female body invoking heat of passion and love. A loved one. The gentle walk of a woman. A pot used for boiling liquids.

~~~~~~~~~~~~~~~~~~~~~~~~~

071 ⚥⊏ **DH   back and forth movement --Dart:** The back and forth rapid flight of a bird.

~~~~~~~~~~~~~~~~~~~~~~~~~

074 ⊞⊏ **DHh   door of the wall -- Push:** The door is pushed to the side to enter. A thrusting of something.

~~~~~~~~~~~~~~~~~~~~~~~~~

077 Ш⊏ **DK   movement in a cup -- Mortar:** Seeds are placed in a stone bowl called a mortar, the stone pestle is used to crush the seeds into a powder. A trampling to crush.

~~~~~~~~~~~~~~~~~~~~~~~~~

078 ⨍⊏ **DL   door on a staff -- Door:** The tent door was hung down as a curtain, covering the entrance to the tent, from a horizontal pole (staff). The door was then moved to the side for going in and out of the tent. Any object that dangles such as a bucket that is hung from a rope down a well to retrieve water. The hair hangs from the head. A poor or weak person hangs the head in poverty. Anything that dangles down and swings back and forth, such as a bucket, branch from a tree or a door.

~~~~~~~~~~~~~~~~~~~~~~~~~

079 〰🝨 **DM** **movement of water -- Blood:** The grape plant takes water from the ground and moves it to the fruit where the water becomes the blood of the grape. The blood of man is also water, which moves through the body. When the blood is shed, the man or animal becomes silent. The color red, the color of blood, man and the earth. A son from the blood of his father resembles his father.

080 🝨 **DN** **door of life -- Rule:** The goal of one who rules or judges is to bring a pleasant and righteous life to the people. An quarrel requiring the need of a ruler or judge to mediate the incident. A deliverer as one who brings life to his people.

081 🝨 **DS** **? -- Myrtle**

082 🝨 **DGh** **door of the eye -- See:** Through the eyes one experiences his world and learns from it. One who has knowledge is one who has experience.

083 🝨 **DPh** **door opened -- Push:** The door is opened by pushing it aside.

084 ∿ᴛ **DTs** **movement to the side -- Leap:** A leap to the side.

~~~~~~~~~~~~~~~~

085 ⊶ᴛ **DQ** **way out of the sun -- Roof:** The roof of the tent provides protection from the heat of the sun.

~~~~~~~~~~~~~~~~

086 𐤓ᴛ **DR** **movement of man -- Circle:** A man is born, comes to maturity, marries and gives birth to sons, repeating the cycle of life. A circling around as the flight of a bird or a dance. Each generation expands the size of the family. The repetitious rhythmic running of a horse.

~~~~~~~~~~~~~~~~

087 �ᴛ **DSh** **back and forth pressing -- Tread:** The treading out of the grain for removing the hulls from the grain. What comes from the grains.

~~~~~~~~~~~~~~~~

088 †ᴛ **DT** **enter a mark -- Covenant:** When two parties agree to follow the terms of a covenant, a mark is given as a sign of continued allegiance.

~~~~~~~~~~~~~~~~

090 ᴍᴴ **HBh** **behold the house -- Gift:** One does not choose the household which one is born into, including tribe, parents, children and wife (as marriages were often arranged by the father), it is a gift from God. These gifts are seen as a privilege and are to be cherished and protected. The expressions and actions toward the family that one was privileged with.

~~~~~~~~~~~~~~~~

091 ᴸᵠ HG great burden -- Meditate: a murmuring or soft speech, for the removal of a burden.

~~~~~~~~~~~~~~~~

092 ⊓ᵠ HD ? -- Shout: When shouting the hands are put up to the mouth. A splendor as something that shouts out

~~~~~~~~~~~~~~~~

093 ᵠᵠ HH arms extended out -- Look: When one sees a great site close by or in the distance, he extends his arms out and sighs as if saying, "ah, look at that" or "behold". A looking toward a breath taking sight or action. A sigh of desire. He or she as one who is pointed at. A sigh of pain.

~~~~~~~~~~~~~~~~

095 ᴄᵠ HZ ? -- Dream

~~~~~~~~~~~~~~~~

100 ᴶᵠ HL looking toward -- Star: The looking toward a light in the distance. The stars have always been used to guide the traveler or shepherd to find his home or destination. When the shepherd has been out

135

in the wilderness with his flock all day and is returning home in the dark, he can see his tent from a great distance because of the glow of the fires, he knows that here is the comfort, safety, and love of the family as well as food and water. To cause a shining of one by praising or giving thanks to another or to ones self.

~~~~~~~~~~~~~~~~~~~~~~~~~

101 ᴍᴪ   HM   the water -- Sea: A large body of water seen as a place of chaos because of its storms, turbulent surf and the commotion of the waves. An uproar. An abundance of something.

~~~~~~~~~~~~~~~~~~~~~~~~~

102 ᴪ   HN   ? -- Heavy: Heavy or abundant in wealth.

~~~~~~~~~~~~~~~~~~~~~~~~~

103 ᴪ   HS   ? -- Still

~~~~~~~~~~~~~~~~~~~~~~~~~

108 ᴪ   HR   the head -- Hill: A mountain or hill as the head rising up above the landscape.

~~~~~~~~~~~~~~~~~~~~~~~~~

110 ᴪ   HT   ? -- Break in

~~~~~~~~~~~~~~~~~~~~~~~~~

116 YY   **WW   two tent pegs -- Pegs:** The tent peg is a "y" shaped wooden peg, which is driven into firm soil. The tent ropes were attached to these pegs, the "y" shape prevents the rope from slipping off the peg.

134 ⊔⊏   **ZBh   food of the house -- Yellow:** The yellow grain is the main staple of the house used for making breads. Any yellow thing such as gold or an animal. Puss as a yellow discharge.

135 ⌐⊏   **ZG   harvest by foot -- Grapeskin:** The juice of the grape is removed/harvested by treading on them in a vat leaving the grapeskins behind.

136 ⊓⊏   **ZD   food at the door -- Soup:** The tent fire located near the door is used for boiling water and making soups.

137 ⊗⊏   **ZH   ? -- This:** Something that stands out or is pointed out.

139 ⊏⊏   **ZZ   great harvesting -- Wealth:** The sickle, a harvesting tool, is swung back and forth cutting the stalks of grain. The stalks are gathered together and stored for future use. A moving back and forth from a fixed location.

~~~~~~~~~~~~~~~~~~~~~~

140 ⊐⊏ **ZHh** **? -- Loose**

~~~~~~~~~~~~~~~~~~~~~~

143 Ѡ⊏ **ZK** **? -- Glass:** A glass without impurities is transparent and pure.

~~~~~~~~~~~~~~~~~~~~~~

144 ✓⊏ **ZL** **cut the staff -- Shake:** A staff is made by cutting a branch from the tree, this green branch shakes and bends easily until it has hardened. (see Isaiah 18.5) A shaking out for removal. The neighing of a horse usually accompanied with the shaking of the head.

~~~~~~~~~~~~~~~~~~~~~~

145 ∿⊏ **ZM** **harvest chaos --** **Plan:** The thoughts and plans that bring about chaos.

~~~~~~~~~~~~~~~~~~~~~~

146 ⤵⊏ **ZN** **mattock of the seed -- Harvest:** One of the many agricultural tools was a hoe or mattock. This implement had a wide blade for cutting a plant stalks at the roots. The crops were harvested for a supply of foods, which were stored in jars. Any implement or object that is broad. The broad ear for picking up sounds. A good supply of food from the harvest will keep the family nourished.

148 ⟨glyph⟩ **ZGh** **harvest experience -- Tremble:** The hard work of the summer harvest brings sweat and exhaustion.

149 ⟨glyph⟩ **ZPh** **? -- Tar:** A pitch used for sealing boats.

151 ⟨glyph⟩ **ZQ** **? -- Bind:** The arms or feet are bound with chains. The binding of different metals to form alloys.

152 ⟨glyph⟩ **ZR** **harvest of heads -- Winnow:** after the grain has been harvested and the heads of grain have been broken open, the heads are thrown into the wind where the chaff is blown away and the seed falls to the ground where they can be gathered. The span of the hand with the fingers spread out. A scattering.

154 ⟨glyph⟩ **ZT** **harvested marker -- Olive:** The oil from the olive fruit was used as an anointing oil for those to hold a kingly or priestly office. The oil is also used as a medicinal ointment.

156 ⌶⌷ㅠ **HhBh wall of the house -- Refuge:** The walls of the house enclose the home as refuge for the family. A refuge functions a place of hiding from any undesirable person or situation.

157 Ḻㅠ **HhG surround and gather -- Festival:** The participants of a festival would gather together and dance in a circle.

158 ⊤ㅠ **HhD wall door -- Unite:** A wall seperates the inside from the outside. Only through the door can one enter or exit uniting the inside with the outside. A uniting together. A parable is a story that brings unity between the hearer and the listener, but the actual meaning is not understood causing a division between the two.

159 ⵰ㅠ **HhH wall reveals -- Life:** The family camp is comprised of many tents, which are laid out in a circle forming a wall of tents. One approaching this wall knows that there is an abundance of life within.

161 ⌐ㅠ **HhZ wall of the harvest -- Watch:** The crops are enclosed by a wall which is watched and guarded against intruders. The family carefully watches and guards the property, livestock and crops.

162 ▥▥ **HhHh great wall -- Thistle:** The wall around crops or livestock was constructed on thistles or rocks with thistles laid on top. The thorns prevented intruders from entering. A hook as a sharp point.

163 ⊗▥ **HhTh ? -- Cord:** Cords are used for binding as well as measuring. A cord is also used as measuring device by placing knots incrementally. The cord is stretched between the two points to measure and the knots are counted.

165 ᐰ▥ **HhK wall of the cup -- Pallette:** The curved roof of the mouth is divided by a ridge or wall. When the mouth is dry the tongue sticks to the roof of the mouth causing the speaker to wait to speak.

166 ᐟ▥ **HhL ? -- Bore:** A hole is drilled with a tool called a bow drill. The string of the bow is wrapped around the drill. By moving the bow back and forth, and firmly pressing down, the drill spins around drilling the hole. The drilling takes patience as the process takes time. Rust bores through metal. Sick as a spinning of the insides. The spinning around in joy. An army bores through the enemy by strongly pressing in.

167 ᴍᴍᴄ HhM   separate water -- Cheese: Cheese was made by placing milk in a bag made out of the skin of an animal. The bag was hung out in the sun and pushed back and forth. The combination of the heat, churning and the natural enzymes in the leather of the bag caused the fat (curds) and water (whey) to separate. The whey could be drunk and the curds eaten or stored for future consumption.

168 ᴺᴄ HhN   tent wall continues -- Camp: A nomads camp consists of many family tents which make up the clan camp. The camp can have as many as fifty tents or more in it. The tents are placed in a circular configuration, forming one continuous wall surrounding the camp. Within this wall is the family clan, a place of freedom, compassion and beauty. The first step to setting up the tent is to arrange the poles. The tent poles were sharpened at one end (and could be used as a weapon) and were driven into the ground. An encampment of tents.

169 ᴄ HhS   wall for holding -- Support: The fabric of the tent walls are supported by the ropes and poles, just as one person who is weak is supported by (leans on, trusts) another who is strong. One is supported by his family line.

171 ᴄ HhPh   wall opened -- Cover: The tent is opened to allow one into its covering for protection. A secret is something that is covered and hidden. A haven as a place covered over for protection.

~~~~~~~~~~~~~~~~~~~~~~~~~~~

172 ⌒⌒⊞ **HhTs** **separation of sides -- Tent Wall:** The tent wall divides or separates the inside from the outside. Here the family resides in privacy and protection from the elements of wind, rain and sun. An arrow divides the flesh.

~~~~~~~~~~~~~~~~~~~~~~~~~~~

173 -●-⊞ **HhQ** **separation and coming together -- Appointment:** The time between the present and an appointment is a wall of time, the closer one gets to the appointment the smaller the wall gets. The appointment is inscribed so that both parties have a reminder of the coming event. The writing is fixed to the tablet as the event is fixed in time.

~~~~~~~~~~~~~~~~~~~~~~~~~~~

174 ⋂⊞ **HhR** **outside man -- Heat:** A man outside in the desert sun becomes pale and hot. Rather than work in the heat of the sun, one waits until the breeze of the day. The wages earned for the work. Anger as a hot emotion. A bleaching by the sun.

~~~~~~~~~~~~~~~~~~~~~~~~~~~

175 ⊔⊔⊞ **HhSh** **wall presses -- Hurry:** The wall, an army or other attacker, advances for destruction. A stillness in the midst of turmoil.

176 †ᴍ   HhT   ? -- Terror

178 ⌐⊗   ThBh   surround the house -- Good: The house is surrounded by grace, beauty, love, health and prosperity.

180 ᴛᴅ⊗   ThD   ? -- Thorn

181 ⁙⊗   ThH   basket seen -- Broom: The fibers of the broom plant were course and strong and used to make brooms. The fibers were also woven and spun into other products such as baskets.

184 ᴍ⊗   ThHh   contain   the   wall   --   Grind: Limestone was ground into a powder. The powder was mixed with water to and used as a strong and durable plaster for coating walls and floors. Limestone was ingested to calm an upset stomach.

185 ⊗⊗   ThTh   contain -- Basket: The basket or bowl, made of clay or wicker, was used for storing foods and other supplies in the nomadic tent. Clay as a common material for constructing baskets, pots and bowls is clay.

188 ↓⊗   **ThL**   **? -- Dew:** A covering over of an area. The spots that cover a lamb's fleece. The hammering of a metal into a sheet to cover wood, an overlay.

189 ⋙⊗   **ThM**   **container of water -- Unclean:** A bowl of water is used to wash dirt off.

190 ↘⊗   **ThN**   **basket continues -- Weave:** A tapestry or basket as woven items.

192 �𝄾⊗   **ThGh**   **? -- Wander**

193 ⊂⊗   **ThPh**   **? -- Trip:** A tripping around like children.

196 ⌂⊗   **ThR**   **surround man -- Wall:** A wall that surrounds one for protection or as a jail. The closing of the doors to the wall.

197 ⊔⊗   **ThSh**   **? -- Pounce**

~~~~~~~~~~~~~~~~~~~~~~~~~~~~~~~~

200 ⊔⤳   **? -- Cry**

~~~~~~~~~~~~~~~~~~~~~~~~~~~~~~~~

202 ⊓⤳   **YD**   **hand moves -- Work:** The hand is the part of the body that enables man to perform many works. With it he can throw away or grab hold, kill or heal, make or destroy. A shout is done by throwing the hands up to the mouth for amplifying. The throwing out of the hand for throwing, praising or thanking.

~~~~~~~~~~~~~~~~~~~~~~~~~~~~~~~~

211 ᗰ⤳   **YM**   **working water -- Sea:** The sea or other large body of water is the place of storms and heavy surf. Considered a place of chaos and terror. The day ends and the new day begins when the sun sets in the west, over the Mediterranean sea.

~~~~~~~~~~~~~~~~~~~~~~~~~~~~~~~~

212 ↘⤳   **YN**   **? -- Wine**

~~~~~~~~~~~~~~~~~~~~~~~~~~~~~~~~

214 ⊜⤳   **YGh**   **? -- Shovel**

~~~~~~~~~~~~~~~~~~~~~~~~~~~~~~~~

218 ᕍ⤳   **YR**   **hand of man -- Throw:** The hand of man is used for the throwing. A flowing of water in a river. A throwing of the finger to show a direction to walk or live. The throwing of an arrow. The throwing down of water in rain. Awe or fear where one throws himself at the foot of one in authority.

~~~~~~~~~~~~~~~~~~~~~~~~

222 ㅁ山 **KBh** **bend the inside -- Pain:** A pain as a fire that causes the insides to bend. The stars appear as fires in the sky.

~~~~~~~~~~~~~~~~~~~~~~~~

224 ㅜ山 **KD** **? -- Jar**

~~~~~~~~~~~~~~~~~~~~~~~~

225 ㅸ山 **KH** **? -- Dark**

~~~~~~~~~~~~~~~~~~~~~~~~

228 ㅍ山 **KHh** **tame the outside -- Strength:** Through strong word the land and animals are tamed to produce crops and livestock. An animal is tamed through chastisement.

~~~~~~~~~~~~~~~~~~~~~~~~

232 ✔山 **KL** **tame for the yoke -- Complete:** An animal or land that is tamed has been worked and is complete and ready for use. Taming include; construction of holding pens, putting the soil to the plow, harvesting of crops, milk or meat. One eats once the harvest is complete. The ability to do the work.

233 ᴍᴍᵁᴶ **KM** ? -- **Desire**

234 ᐱᵁᴶ **KN** **opening of a seed -- Root:** When the seed opens the roots begin to form the base of the plant by going down into the soil. The plant rises out of the ground forming the stalk of the plant. A tall tree can only stand tall and firm because of the strong root system which supports it. A firm or sure position. A priest as one who stands firm between God and the nation. Words or names that are given in support of another.

235 ᐊᵁᴶ **KS** **palm that grabs hold -- Cup:** The curved palm covers, holds and hides the contents inside it. Any type of covering. A bag or pocket. A seat that is covered by the sitter. To cover a group by counting.

237 ᴄᵁᴶ **KPh** **palm open -- Palm:** The curved shape of the open hand. Any curved or hollowed out object. The placing of the palm on something and pressing down or pushing. The bending of the will of an animal.

239 ᴏᵁᴶ **KQ** ? -- **Caterpillar**

240 ꤩꟺ **KR** **bent man -- Leap:** One bends down before leaping. Also for digging. A farm as a place where one digs the ground for growing crops. A bowl as an hollowed out object. The wall of a trench that is dug out.

242 ✝ꟺ **KT** **cover the covenant -- Crush:** The crushing of the olives produce olive oil, used as a covering for ceremonial purposes.

244 ꤓꟙ **LBh** **authority inside -- Heart:** The consciousness of man is seen as coming from deep inside the chest, the heart. Thirst as an Inside desire for water.

245 ꤡꟙ **LG** **? -- Study**

246 ꤍꟙ **LD** **? -- Child:** The bearing of children.

247 ꤚꟙ **LH** **great yoke -- Weary:** An young oxen unaccustomed to the weight and operation of the yoke becomes tired. A work that comes to nothing. A joining to the yoke. An ornamentation placed on the neck as a yoke.

249 ↰↵ **LZ** **authority cut -- Turn aside:** A turning away from truth.

250 ↰↵ **LHh** **tongue outside -- Moist:** When the lips are dry, the tongue licks the lips to moisten them. Anything that is moist or fresh. A common writing material is wet clay. The letters can be easily inscribed and the clay hardens to preserve the record.

251 ⊗↵ **LTh** **authority contained -- Veil:** A covering to hide the face. The camouflaging capability of the lizard to hide.

253 ↰↵ **LK** **staff in the palm -- Walk:** A nomad traveled on foot with a staff in his hand to provide support in walking as well as a weapon to defend against predators or thief's. A messenger as one who walks for another

254 ↵↵ **LL** **? -- Night:** When the night comes, the night sky is rolled out like a scroll. When daylight comes, the night sky is rolled up like a scroll. A stairway that rolls around itself. The sound of the wolf, a night predator.

255 ᴍ𝓤 **LM**   **staff of might -- Staff:** The shepherd always carried his staff for guiding, leading and protecting the flock. The flock was bound to the shepherd, as the staff was a sign of his authority over the sheep. The yoke was a staff laid across the shoulders of two oxen. The oxen were then tied to the yokes at the neck, binding the two together for plowing or pulling a cart. A people bound together. A wound bound with bandages.

256 ᒾ𝓤 **LN**   **bound continually -- Remain:** To remain in a place or position for a long duration.

258 ⊘𝓤 **LGh**   **tongue seen -- Throat:** When looking down the throat you see the tongue. A swallowing. The blurting out of words coming from the throat rather than the heart.

259 ⊘𝓤 **LPh**   **? -- Stick**

260 ᴀ𝓤 **LTs**   **tongue of trouble -- Mock**

264 ᥔ𝓤 **LSh**   **? -- Knead**

267 ᒪ᭙ᚈ **MG** **water carries -- Disolve:** The washing away by water. A fainting or melting.

268 ᐪᚈ᭙ **MD** **water at the door -- Carpet:** A carpet was stretched out to cover the dirt floor of the tent. A bowl of water was located at the door so that one could wash his feet before stepping on the carpet. Just as the carpet is stretched out to cover the floor, the garments worn by the nomad is stretched out to cover the body. Also, a string is stretched out for measuring.

269 ᛩ᭙ **MH** **water behold -- Sea:** The sea (Mediterranean) is a place of the unknown (what is beyond or what is below). It is feared by the Ancient Hebrews because of its size, storms and fierceness. Anything that is unknown or a question to find the unknown (who, what, when, where, why, how). A hundred as an unknowable amount.

271 ᐱᚈ᭙ **MZ** **mighty harvest -- Barn:** A storage facility for the harvest. The stomach as a storage place for food.

272 ᚊᚈ᭙ **MHh** **liquid inside -- Marrow:** The marrow is a buttery liquid inside the bones and is used as a choice food. To obtain the marrow, the bone must be struck to break it open.

~~~~~~~~~~~~~~~~~~~~~~

273 ⊗ᴍ   **MTh   liquid contained -- Branch:** A green branch still contains water allowing the branch to be flexible. The yoke is cut green then shaped to the desired shape and left to dry.

~~~~~~~~~~~~~~~~~~~~~~

275 Ⱳᴍ   **MK   might subdued -- Low:** Something brought low in submission, humility or wealth.

~~~~~~~~~~~~~~~~~~~~~~

276 ᴠᴍ   **ML   ? -- Reduce:** The reduction of quantity or quality. Sickness as a reduction in health. A reduction by being cut off. Yesterday and what is before as a time cut off.

~~~~~~~~~~~~~~~~~~~~~~

277 ᴍᴍ   **MM   great chaos -- nothing:** Anything that is considered useless or without value. A blemish that causes something to be valueless.

~~~~~~~~~~~~~~~~~~~~~~

278 ᴺᴍ   **MN   blood continues -- Kind:** Each species (kind) continues by passing its blood to the following generation which comes from the parent. A large group of the same kind are stronger than one. Refusal as a strength of the will. An assigning of a group

153

together who are of the same kind. Those of the same kind, look alike. The right hand as the strong hand.

~~~~~~~~~~~~~~~~~~~~~

279 𐤌𐤌 **MS** **water grabs hold -- Disolve:** The dissolving or melting away of something. Fainting is a dissolving of the inside. A spurning as dissolving away of another.

~~~~~~~~~~~~~~~~~~~~~

280 𐤏𐤌 **MGh** **? -- Bowels**

~~~~~~~~~~~~~~~~~~~~~

282 𐤑𐤌 **MTs** **? -- Chaff:** The seed is thrown on the threshing floor, the oxen trample over the seeds, putting them under pressure forcing the seed out of the hull (chaff). A sucking as a pressing with the lips.

~~~~~~~~~~~~~~~~~~~~~

283 𐤒𐤌 **MQ** **water expands -- Dissipate:** When water is poured out on the ground it dissipates. A mocking, as a dissipating of another.

~~~~~~~~~~~~~~~~~~~~~

284 𐤓𐤌 **MR** **water head -- Bitter:** The headwaters of a river are only a trickle and have stagnant pools causing the water to be bitter. Rebellion is one with a bitter attitude. The headwaters may also be a life-giving source of water in the desert. The headwaters of a river have very low flow where water collects in holes or pools.

Because of the lack of flow it is bitter tasting. Words may be spoken as bitter or sweet. An exchange as a going one-way to another.

~~~~~~~~~~~~~~~~~~~~~~~

285 ⊔⊔ᴧᴧ **MSh** **? -- Draw out**

~~~~~~~~~~~~~~~~~~~~~~~

286 †ᴧᴧ **MT** **chaos mark -- Death**

~~~~~~~~~~~~~~~~~~~~~~~

288 ⊔ᑊ **NBh** **seed inside -- Germinate:** A seed opens and the plant bores through the soil to the surface. The plant rises and produces fruit. A prophecy is a germinating of words that will bring about fruit.

~~~~~~~~~~~~~~~~~~~~~~~

289 ᒪᑊ **NG** **? -- Bright**

~~~~~~~~~~~~~~~~~~~~~~~

290 ⊓ᑊ **ND** **continue back and forth -- Shake:** A back and forth movement such as the shaking of the head or the quivering of the lips. A removal or fleeing for a time such as during menstruation.

~~~~~~~~~~~~~~~~~~~~~~~

291 ⛨ᑊ **continue the breath -- Sit:** The continual sitting or dwelling in one place for any reason. A driving out of another people to sit in their place.

293 ⌐╲   NZ   ? -- **Sprinkle**

294 ⊓╲   NHh   ? -- **Rest:** The shepherd would guide his flock to a place of water. Here is water for drinking as well as green grass for pasturing. Once the flock arrives, they are free to rest after the long journey. A guided journey to a place of rest. A sigh of rest.

295 ⊗╲   NTh   seed in a basket -- **Settle:** Seeds from the harvest were placed in baskets for storage. When the basket is shaken, the seeds spread out flat allowing for more room for the seeds.

297 ⊎╲   NK   continue the palm -- **Beat:** A continued beating with the palm plays the drum.

298 ∪╲   NL   ? -- **Complete**

299 ⋁⋁╲   NM   ? -- **Drowsy:** The state of unconsciousness that allows speech from the heart.

300 ꙄꙄ   **NN**   **seed of seed -- Continue:** The seed is the continuation of life from the parent plant. This cycle continues generation after generation.

---

301 ꙄꙄ   **NS**   **continue to grab hold -- Flag:** The tribal flag or standard that is hung from a horizontal pole, which is attached to a vertical pole such as a sail. The flag, or standard, is lifted up to be seen from a distance. The flag as the place of refuge that one flees to. Something that is lifted up or exalted.

---

302 ꙄꙄ   **NGh**   **? -- Rattle:** A shaking.

---

303 ꙄꙄ   **NPh**   **continual edge -- Region:** The border that encircles an area.

---

304 ꙄꙄ   **NTs**   **? -- Despise:** A quarrel.

---

305 ꙄꙄ   **NQ**   **life drawn in -- Suckle:** The innocent cry of a baby when hungry.

---

306 𐤍𐤓 **NR** **seed beginning -- Plow:** Rains in the mountainous areas cause a flooding of the rivers. The rivers swell causing the water to flood the land next to the river. This is the only water that the land will see and is necessary for crop production. After the flood season, the land is plowed by the use of a plow attached to the yoke of the oxen. While the surface is dry, the turned up soil glistens in the sun from the water remaining in the soil. This water is necessary for the seed to begin germination. A lampstand also brings forth light.

307 𐤔𐤍 **NSh** **continual pressing -- Debt:** A debt or loan that causes pressure or sickness. A deception that brings one indebted to another.

310 𐤎𐤁 **SBh** **turning of the inside -- Dizzy:** One drunk from strong drink, turns from dizziness. The old, gray haired ones, easily become dizzy.

311 𐤎𐤂 **SG** **? -- Increase**

312 𐤎𐤃 **SD** **? -- Foundation:** A level piece of ground is found for setting up the tent. The elders are the foundation of the community who make decrees. The floor of permanent homes were sometimes covered with a lime plaster for a smooth floor. A witness brings an account to the elders who meet on the floor of the tent for rulings. A level field of ground. A limestone plaster is made for the floor of buildings to form a smooth and level surface.

~~~~~~~~~~~~~~~~~~~~~~

313 𝕏𝕏 **SH** **protector reveals -- Veil:** The veil is lifted to reveal the face that is hidden. The lifting of oneself in pride.

~~~~~~~~~~~~~~~~~~~~~~

316 𝕏𝕏 **SHh** **thorn wall -- Pond:** The edge of the pond is a wall of plants. The pond provides a quiet and serene place for meditation. A place for swimming and bathing. The floating on the water or one floating in meditation. One who sits by the pond to ponder as a plant sits by the water. The growth around a pond.

~~~~~~~~~~~~~~~~~~~~~~

317 𝕏𝕏 **STh** **turn around -- Turn aside**

~~~~~~~~~~~~~~~~~~~~~~

319 𝕏𝕏 **SK** **protective covering -- Booth:** The watcher over the crops, flock or herd, would construct a covering (booth) as a shelter from the sun, wind or rain. These coverings were often constructed on an elevated position, and from materials readily available such as bushes, thorns and small trees. A wound was covered with olive oil as a medicine.

~~~~~~~~~~~~~~~~~~~~~~

320 ◡≼ **SL** **turn of the staff -- Balance:** A balance scale consisted of a small wooden beam (staff) held in place at the center. At both ends of the beam was attached a tray for placing objects. The object to be weighed would lower. Measured weights were added to the other tray until the tray being weighed raised and became level with the other tray. A rising up of something. After quail land after crossing a large sea they are unable to lift themselves up any longer due to exhaustion. This was a convenient means of gathering meat for the table.

~~~~~~~~~~~~~~~~~~~~

321 ∿≼ **SM** **? -- Store:** A storehouse where stores are put. To set anything in a place.

~~~~~~~~~~~~~~~~~~~~

322 ↘≼ **SN** **protective seed -- Thorn:** A thorn bush can be a blessing or a curse. The desert traveler often comes in contact with these thorns and brushing the leg against them causing pain. The same thorns are used by the shepherd to build a wall (shield) made of these thorn bushes to enclose his flock during the night which will help keep predators out. A wall of thorns for protecting the sheep from wolves. Boots were designed to protect the legs from thorns. Hate as a thorn in the heart.

~~~~~~~~~~~~~~~~~~~~

323 ≼≼ **SS** **great turning -- Turn:** The twisting and turning of a bird in flight or a horse playing.

~~~~~~~~~~~~~~~~~~~~

324 ⊙≼ **SGh**   **? -- Rush**

~~~~~~~~~~~~~~~~

325 ⊂≼ **SPh**   **protection of the mouth -- Lips:** The edge of the mouth. The lips gather the food into the mouth.

~~~~~~~~~~~~~~~~

327 •⊙≼ **SQ**   **? -- Sack**

~~~~~~~~~~~~~~~~

328 ⋒≼ **SR**   **turn the head -- Direct:** The turning of the head to another direction. The yoke, attached to the neck, is used by the driver to turn the head of the ox. A turning around. One who rules turns the people to his direction. The turning the head of the child or student into a particular direction. A fishhook that turns the head of the fish.

~~~~~~~~~~~~~~~~

330 †≼ **ST**   **turn from the covenant -- Provoke:** To lead or provoke another in a different direction.

~~~~~~~~~~~~~~~~

332 ⊔⊙ **GhBh**   **experience the tent -- Dark cover:** The tent is made of a covering of thick and heavy black or dark brown goat hair.

333 L◎   **GhG**   **? -- Cake**

334 ⊤◎   **GhD**   **experienced back and forth --**
Witness: A place, time or event that is repeated again and
again. A testimony is a repeating of an account. An
appointed place, time or event that is repeated.

335 ♀◎   **GhH**   **? -- Ruin:** To bring down in a heap
by twisting.

337 ⌐◎   **GhZ**   **know a weapon -- Bold:** A refuge
as a place for making a firm and fierce stand. A goat
stands firm in its strength.

339 ⊗◎   **GhTh**   **depress around -- Stylus:** When a
bird of prey drops down on its prey, the talons grab hold
of the prey, and firmly presses around it causing the
talons to be buried into the prey. A writing stylus is a
small pointed stick that is pressed into the clay for
inscribing. A tight wrapping around.

342 ↓◎   **GhL**   **experience the staff -- Yoke:** The
yoke, a staff is lifted over the shoulder, is attached to the

oxen for performing work. One taken into exile is placed in the yoke. It was a common practice to strip the clothes off of those taken into exile. Milk is a product from the female oxen. A coat lifted up onto the shoulders.

~~~~~~~~~~~~~~~~~~

343 ᴍᴄᴓ **GhM** **experience the masses -- People:** A group who reside with each other where the masses become as one.

~~~~~~~~~~~~~~~~~~

344 ᴕᴄᴓ **GhN** **continue the eye -- Watch:** The nomadic agriculturalist carefully watches over his livestock and crops by keeping a close eye on them. It was common to construct a shelter consisting of a roof on four posts, as a shelter from the glare of the sun. A furrow depression is formed between the eyes when watching intensely. The furrow may also be formed by concentration or depression. The home is a place closely watched. Protection of the home by keeping of a close eye on it. A bird that intently watches. The eye reveals the heart of the person. A spring or fountain is the eye of the ground.

~~~~~~~~~~~~~~~~~~

345 ᶘᴄᴓ **GhS** **watch and hold on -- Tread:** Grapes are placed in a vat. A rope is suspended from above and is held onto by the grape treaders for support. The making or doing of anything.

~~~~~~~~~~~~~~~~~~

347 ◠◎ **GhPh** **eyes open -- Bird:** A branch as the resting place for the birds. Exhaustion from a long flight.

~~~~~~~~~~~~~~~~~~~~~~~~~~~~

348 ᴧ◎ **GhTs** **? -- Tree:** The upright and firmness of the tree. The spine makes man stand upright and firm. The elders of the tribe were the upright and firm ones making decisions and giving advice.

~~~~~~~~~~~~~~~~~~~~~~~~~~~~

349 ⊸◎ **GhQ** **? -- Press**

~~~~~~~~~~~~~~~~~~~~~~~~~~~~

350 ᕁ◎ **GhR** **watch a man -- Naked:** When the enemy is captured, he is stripped of his clothes to the skin and carefully watched.

~~~~~~~~~~~~~~~~~~~~~~~~~~~~

351 ⊔◎ **GhSh** **? -- Moth**

~~~~~~~~~~~~~~~~~~~~~~~~~~~~

352 †◎ **GhT** **? -- Time**

~~~~~~~~~~~~~~~~~~~~~~~~~~~~

355 Ꝉ◠ **PG** **? -- Unfit:** Unable to fulfill the role intended for. An unripe fig.

~~~~~~~~~~~~~~~~~~~~~~~~~~~~

356 PD   **open the door -- Redeem:** To bring back to an original state.

~~~~~~~~~~~~~~~~~~~~~~~~~~~

357 PH   **mouth of breath -- Mouth:** The mouth is place of speaking and blowing. A mouth is the edge of anything such as the place of the beard, a region (when the Hebrews speak of the border of something they are referring to all that is within the borders) or sword. A place, thing or event that goes beyond the normal such as a miracle, sign, wonder or beauty.

~~~~~~~~~~~~~~~~~~~~~~~~~~~

359 PZ   **edge of the plow -- Refine:** The plow point was the only implement requiring a strong metal refined by fire because of its constant work in the soil and the grazing over rocks.

~~~~~~~~~~~~~~~~~~~~~~~~~~~

360 PHh   **blow to separate -- Spread:** The spreading out dust by blowing on it. The ruler of a spread out area.

~~~~~~~~~~~~~~~~~~~~~~~~~~~

363 PK   **? -- Flask:** The flask stored such materials as cosmetics. The flask is overturned to pour out the contents.

~~~~~~~~~~~~~~~~~~~~~~~~~~~

364 PL **speak to authority -- Intercede:** When one comes before one of authority to intercede for another, he bows low out of respect. A great sight deserving respect. The bent shape of the bean as if bowing before an authority.

365 PM **? -- Fat**

366 PN **? -- Face:** The part of the body that turns. A wheel or other turning object.

367 PS **? -- Wrist:** The end of the extremities including the wrist and ankles.

368 PGh **? -- Viper**

370 PTs **open the side -- Smash:** When something is struck with a maul, it is smashed and the pieces scatter. An opening by force.

371 PQ **? -- Stagger**

372 ⊓⇐ **PR** **open the head -- Tread:** The heads of grains are scattered on the threshing floor, a smooth, hard and level surface. An ox is lead around the floor crushing the heads, opening them to reveal the fruit inside. The winepress is a vat where the grapes are placed and tread on the open the grapes to reveal the juices inside. At the conclusion of the treading, an abundance of fruit is acquired.

373 Ш⇐ **PSh** **? -- Spread**

374 †⇐ **PT** **open mark -- Socket:** The hinges of a door were made by a hole placed in the door jam. The door was made with a rods which were set into the hole, allowing the door to swivel in the socket. A hole dug in the ground for capturing.

376 ⊔⊐⌒ **TsBh** **side of the tent -- Wall:** The walls of the tent enclose what is inside. The tent walls stand firm and strong, protecting it from the harsh elements. As the family swells in size, the tent walls are enlarged. An army as a wall of protection.

377 ⌐⌒ **TsG** **? -- Set:** A placing in a specific location.

378 ⊓o∧ **TsD**   **side movement -- Side:** One lays down to sleep, hide or ambush.

379 ⍦o∧ **TsH**   **hunt for revelation -- Landmark:** The desert nomad's existence depended on water and pasture for the flocks and would migrate from one location to another. Landmarks, such as rivers, wadi's, mountain ranges, rock outcroppings, valleys, etc. are the familiar and known markers by which the nomad guides the migration. Like the nomad, the ship follows the stars as landmarks to their destination. Through the journey along the road of life, there are certain requirements, directions and remembrances, which must be observed and followed to live a right and prosperous life. It was the responsibility of the father to teach the landmarks of the terrain as well as the landmarks of a right life.

382 ⊞o∧ **TsHh**   **trouble outside -- Desert:** A hot and dry place from the glaring of the sun. A crying out from thirst.

386 ↵o∧ **TsL**   **? -- Shade:** A place of shadows. A hiding in the shadows.

387 ᴍᴀᴧ **TsM**   **hunt for water -- Thirst:** A fasting from water, or food.

~~~~~~~~~~~~~~~~

388 ᴦᴀᴧ **TsN**   **? -- Thorn:** The sharp piercing thorns that cause pain as well as protection. The thorn bushes were often used by the shepherd to build a corral for the flock sheep. The thorns would deter any predators.

~~~~~~~~~~~~~~~~

390 ᴑᴀᴧ **TsGh**   **laying known -- Bed:** The bed consisted of blankets spread out on the floor of the tent. A spreading out of something.

~~~~~~~~~~~~~~~~

391 ᴑᴀᴧ **TsPh**   **lay down the mouth -- Whisper:** The guards quietly whisper to each other to prevent detection.

~~~~~~~~~~~~~~~~

392 ᴀᴧᴀᴧ **TsTs**   **? -- Blossom:** The function of the blossom is to produce the fruit of the tree.

~~~~~~~~~~~~~~~~

393 ᴏ-ᴀᴧ **TsQ**   **sides coming together -- Funnel:** Used for pouring.

~~~~~~~~~~~~~~~~

394 ᚈᚐ TsR hunted man -- Pressed: A man being chased goes to a place of refuge and defense such as a rock outcropping where clefts in the rocks allow for concealment. A cleft is a tight place where the man presses himself in. The rocks can also be used as weapons by throwing them or fashioning them into knives. The flint knife is made of a glassy type rock that fractures evenly when struck or firmly pressed in the proper place and angle. Something that is stored by being wrapped up tightly. A belt as wrapped around the middle tightly. The olives are pressed to extract the glimmering oil. Being pressed in a narrow tight place.

396 ᛏᚐ TsT ? -- Kindle

398 QBh surround the inside -- Jar: A container for storing. The stomach as a jar inside of man that stores food.

400 QD ? -- Bow: The bowing down of the head.

401 QH ? -- Cord: The Cord is used to secure items together or for attaching to an object to make a sling.

404 ▥-●-   **QHh**   **?** -- **Take:** Merchandise as taken.

~~~~~~~~~~~~~~~~~~~~~~~~

405 ⊗-●-   **QTh**   **?** -- **Little:** Something that is little or made little by cutting off.

~~~~~~~~~~~~~~~~~~~~~~~~

408 ∿-●-   **QL**   **gathering**   **to**   **the**   **staff**   -- **Shepherd:** The Shepherd traveled light. He carried with him a long staff for directing the sheep as well as to protect them from predators. The shepherd also carried a bag, which included some food supplies. The sheep knew the voice of their shepherd. When it came time to move he would call them and they would quickly gather to him. The light supplies of the shepherd or a swift traveler.

~~~~~~~~~~~~~~~~~~~~~~~~

409 ∿-●-   **QM**   **?** -- **Raise:** A rising or standing of anything.

~~~~~~~~~~~~~~~~~~~~~~~~

410 ↘-●-   **QN**   **gathering for the seeds** -- **Nest:** The gathering of materials by the parent for building a nest for the seeds (eggs). The parent bird will guard over and protect the nest and eggs from predators. Man can guard over the family, wife, and possessions in a positive way (protect, from an enemy) or in a negative way (by not trusting or a desire to have another's possessions). The process of gathering branches for the nest; mans gathering or acquiring materials by taking or buying. The Ancients measured wealth by the amount of one's possessions and measured distances using a branch with marks on it. The striking of a musical note as a bird sings in the nest. The bringing forth of chicks into the nest. The singing of the bird in the nest.

411 QS ? -- **Scales:** The scales of a fish.

412 QGh ? -- **Gash:** A mark by branding, incision, tattoo or dislocation.

413 QPh sun speaks -- **Seasons:** As the sun travels through the sky it marks (speaks, commands) the times and seasons (see Genesis 1:14). The condensing of the light at the sun when at the horizons, a condensing of milk into curdles. A going around of the sun from one horizon to the other.

414 QTs ? -- **Cut:** Making the end of something by cutting it off. An ending of sleep. Harvesting of the crops by cutting.

416 QR gather the men -- **Meeting:** The men often came together during the cool of the day to discuss the news of the camp. A calling together for assembly. The meeting or bringing together of people or objects by arrangement, accident or purchase.

~~~~~~~~~~~~~~~~~~~

417 ⊔⊔-● **QSh** **bring together and pressed --**
Straw: Once the straw is harvested from the field, it is gathered into bundles and secured with a cord in the middle. While the middle is firmly pressed together, the top and bottom bend outward. The snare is constructed of a bent branch and tied to the trap.

~~~~~~~~~~~~~~~~~~~

420 �換 **RBh** **head of the family -- Judge:** Each tribe had judges who ruled cases, trials, conflicts and contests. This person was the representative for the whole tribe, one abundant in authority and wisdom (see Exodus 18:25).

~~~~~~~~~~~~~~~~~~~

421 ⌊ᕼ **RG** **man foot -- Trample:** The treading underfoot of something, possibly accompanied by a loud noise and the breaking of something. Something that is bad is trampled on. A woven rug that is laid on the floor of the tent for walking on. The walking over one with the intent to kill.

~~~~~~~~~~~~~~~~~~~

422 ⊓ᕼ **RD** **head hanging -- Wander:** A walking or treading where the head is hanging or looking down. The treaders in the winepress look at their step while trampling on the grapes. One aimlessly walking and

looking at his feet. Whenever climbing or walking down a
steep grade, one watches his step carefully.

~~~~~~~~~~~~~~~~~~~~~~~~~

423 ⲫⲛ   **RH**   **man beholds -- See**

~~~~~~~~~~~~~~~~~~~~~~~~~

425 ⲣⲛ   **RZ**   **? -- Ceder:** The bark of the ceder is
pulled off in thin thread like fibers. The strength of cedar
wood.

~~~~~~~~~~~~~~~~~~~~~~~~~

426 ⲙⲛ   **RHh**   **man   outside   --   Path:** The
responsibilities of the nomad outside of the tent include
the feeding, watering and caring for the livestock.
Livestock are healthier and more productive when on a
routine, therefore the man follows a routine or "a
prescribed path" each day when caring for his livestock. A
traveler follows a prescribed path to arrive at a specific
destination. The Ancient handmill consisted of two round
stones, called millstones; the top was turned on top of the
other to grind the grain. This top stone always followed
the same path on top of the other. The Hebrew nomads
were very familiar with the wind patterns, as they would
follow a prescribed path indicating the coming season.
From this word comes the idea of breath, as it is the wind
of man, which also follows a prescribed path of inhaling
and exhaling. The moon follows a prescribed path each
night from horizon to horizon. A smell that is carried by
the wind and smelled while breathing.

~~~~~~~~~~~~~~~~~~~~~~~~~

427 ⊗ℕ   **RTh**   **top of a container -- Trough:** The digging out of something for making a basin or trough. A trembling as a hollowing out of the insides.

429 ᴟℕ   **RK**   **man covered -- Loins:** The loins of a man is the area around the waist and upper thighs and is always covered. Future generations come out of the loins of the father. The thigh is the longest bone in the body.

431 ᴟℕ   **RM**   **? -- Lift:** Anything that is high or lifted up.

432 ᴟℕ   **RN**   **? -- Shout:** Any loud noise or instrument.

433 ᴟℕ   **RS**   **top grabbed -- Break down:** The breaking or bringing down of something by pulling it down.

434 ⊙ℕ   **RGh**   **man watched -- Companion:** The shepherd closely watched over his flock, often they are his only companion.

435 ⌐ᕓ **RPh man open -- Wound:** Plant material such as seeds, leaves, stalks, flowers, roots, etc, were pulverized into a medicinal paste for applying to wounds or into a powder for internal ingestion.

436 ᕓ **RTs ? -- Potsherd:** Broken pieces of pottery were commonly used as writing tablets as they were inexpensive and durable. Runners carried messages from one to another on potsherds. Land is divided up into sections by tribe or nations.

437 ⌐ᕓ **RQ top drawn together -- Bottle:** The mouth of the bottle, usually made of animal skins, is drawn together with a cord. The liquid is poured out of the mouth. Spit is a liquid that comes out of the mouth of a man. Also green, from the color of spit.

438 ᕓᕓ **RR ? -- Saliva:** Also the white of an egg which is similar in consistency to saliva. A cursing by spitting on another.

439 ᕓ **RSh head of two -- Chief:** The Chief (head of the tribe) is the authority of the tribe. He hears the requests of the tribe, the representative and ruler of the land that he governs and the one who divides up the land

and possessions of the tribe. The head of a person, place, thing or time.

~~~~~~~~~~~~~~~

442 ᴸᴼᴸᴸ **ShB** **press to the tent -- Return:** The return to the tent for rest. A sitting. A return or turning back to another land or place. A captive that is taken back to the land of the captors.

~~~~~~~~~~~~~~~

443 ᴸᴸᴸ **ShG** **double burden -- Mistake:** When a work is found to be in error, the work must be redone. A groan one makes when making a mistake.

~~~~~~~~~~~~~~~

444 ᵀᴸᴸ **ShD** **two that dangle -- Teats:** The goat and sheep have two teats dangling below the udder. The teats provide milk (life) and power to the kids. The ravines of a mountain where water rushes down providing life to the soil.

~~~~~~~~~~~~~~~

445 ᴴᴸᴸ **ShH** **? -- Storm:** The roar and devastation of a storm.

~~~~~~~~~~~~~~~

448 ᴴᴴᴸᴸ **ShHh** **sharp walls -- Pit:** A pit dug into the ground for the purpose of trapping someone or something. Hunger where the stomach is an empty pit.

449 ⊗ᄔ   **ShTh   repeat   around   -- Lash:** Two
objects are lashed together by wrapping a cord around
them. The lashing at or out of someone or something with
a cord or branch. Despise as a lashing out. An oar lashes
out at the water.

451 ᙡᄔ   **ShK   two in the palm -- Testes:** The two
parts in the palm (the curved part) of the loins.

452 ᔑᄔ   **ShL   ? -- Draw out:** The drawing out of
an answer.

453 ᒼᒻ\ᄔ   **ShM   ? -- Breath:** The breath is the life
or character of the person. Hebrew names are words
usually describing their character, reflecting their breath.
The wind is the breath of the sky located high in the
heavens. A wind blowing over the land pulls the moisture
out of the ground drying it up, making a place of ruin or
desert. One in horror or in astonishment is one dried up in
the inside. One who is guilty is in a desolate state.

454 ᔆᄔ   **ShN   teeth of life -- Teeth:** The two
front teeth are sharp and used for cutting foods by

pressing down. Two as a repeating of the first or what was before.

~~~~~~~~~~~~~~~~~~~~~~

455 𐤔 **ShS   Press and grab hold -- Plunder:** The pressing into another's place and grabbing hold of his possessions.

~~~~~~~~~~~~~~~~~~~~~~

456 𐤔 **ShGh destroyer watches -- Shepherd:** The shepherd cares for and delights in his sheep. When the sheep are in the pasture, the shepherd carefully watches over the surrounding area always on the lookout for danger. When a predator comes to attack, the Shepherd destroys the enemy. When the sheep are in trouble they will cry out to the shepherd who will deliver them. The sheep graze in safety in the wide-open pasture. A wide-open and free place or state.

~~~~~~~~~~~~~~~~~~~~~~

457 𐤔 **ShPh   sharp teeth in the mouth -- Serpent:** A serpent (venomous snake) has sharp fangs in the mouth. A quiver as the pouch where the arrows (sharp teeth) are placed in the mouth. A drawing in by swallowing (as the snake swallows its prey) also, to draw in air or water.

~~~~~~~~~~~~~~~~~~~~~~

459 𐤔 **ShQ   repeat a cycle -- River:** During the rain season, repeated each year, the riverbeds become full of water. The surrounding land is soaked with water allowing for the planting of crops. The leg of a river, or a man or street.

~~~~~~~~~~~~~~~~~~~~~~~~~~~~~~

460 ॴԼԼ ShR press the beginning -- Rope: Ropes and cords were usually made of bark strips such as from the cedar or from the sinew (tendon) of an animal. The rope is made by twisting two fibers together. A single fiber is attached to a fixed point (top), and the two ends of the fiber are brought together. One fiber is twisted in a clockwise direction and wrapped over the other fiber in counter clockwise direction. The second fiber is then twisted in clockwise direction then wrapped around the first fiber in a counter clockwise direction. The process is repeated through the length of the rope. The twisting of the fibers in opposite directions causes the fibers to lock (press) onto each other making a stronger rope. The rope is used to tightly secure or support something, such as a load to a cart or the poles of the tent. A cord pulled tight is straight. One who is happy is one whose life is lived straightly. A relative as one from the same umbilical cord of the family. The blood relatives remain with the tent. The loosening of a cord around a load. A traveler may have a wagon pulled by a bull where the load on the cart is secured with a cord. A righteous one is one who is straight and firmly holds up truth just as the cord is straight and firmly holds the wall of the tent upright. A stringed musical instrument uses thin cords for making music.

~~~~~~~~~~~~~~~~~~~~~~~~~~~~~~

461 ԼԼԼԼ ShSh teeth -- White: The whiteness of the teeth. The white hair of the older men.

462 †⊔⊔   **ShT**   **? -- Buttock:** The place of sitting, a foundation. A banquet as a time of sitting together.

464 ⊔⊓†   **TBh**   **sign inside -- Longing:** The inside desire to follow after something.

466 ⊓†   **TD**   **mark the door -- Peg:** When the site of the tent is determined, the location of the door is determined by the father, possibly by using a tent peg as a marker for its location.

467 ⚯†   **TH**   **mark revealed -- Mark:** A marks identifies locations is used to mark out a location. Two crossed sticks in the shape of cross were used to hang the family standard or flag.

469 ⌐†   **TZ**   **mark a cut -- Cut off**

470 ⊓⊓†   **THh**   **? -- Under:** The under or lower part of anything

473 **TK** **mark of the palm -- Bend:** The lines or marks in the center of the palm are formed by the bending of the palm. A bending in the middle, the center of something. A sitting as a bending down.

474 **TL** **? -- Ruin:** The mounds of a ruined city. To bring down to ruin or death, by destruction or deception.

475 **TM** **? -- Full:** What is full is whole and complete. Twins as a full womb. Amazed as a full and overwhelmed mind.

476 **TN** **path continues -- Constant:** A patient and continuous movement. A donkey as a patient and constant animal.

478 **TGh** **? -- Mock**

479 **TPh** **? -- Drum:** The beating of a drum.

481 **TQ** **? -- Ledge**

482 𐤓𐤕 **TR** **mark of man:** The border of the land owned by an individual, or under his control, is marked by markers. An outline or border. To walk to border of the property as owner or spy. An extension of the border.

483 𐤑𐤕 **TSh** **? -- Goat:** The butting of the heads of the goat.

Appendix F – Number Cross References

Strong's Number - Ancient Hebrew Number

0001	002	0084	042	0167	100	0231	134	0334	196
0003	002	0092	048	0168	100	0232	394	0335	005
0006	026	0093	051	0174	100	0233	007	0336	005
0008	026	0095	064	0176	005	0235	144	0337	005
0009	026	0096	056	0178	002	0237	144	0338	005
0010	026	0098	057	0180	034	0238	146	0339	005
0011	026	0099	057	0181	004	0239	146	0340	002
0012	026	0100	057	0182	004	0240	146	0341	002
0013	026	0101	058	0183	005	0241	146	0342	002
0014	027	0102	061	0184	005	0246	151	0343	004
0015	027	0103	064	0185	005	0247	394	0344	005
0016	027	0107	064	0188	005	0251	008	0346	005
0017	027	0108	004	0190	005	0253	008	0349	005
0018	037	0113	080	0191	247	0254	008	0351	005
0019	030	0117	086	0193	012	0255	008	0352	012
0024	002	0119	079	0194	005	0258	158	0353	012
0034	027	0120	079	0196	247	0259	158	0354	012
0035	027	0122	079	0197	255	0260	008	0355	012
0046	042	0124	079	0199	005	0262	159	0360	012
0047	042	0125	079	0199	255	0264	008	0361	012
0055	033	0127	079	0200	247	0268	174	0365	012
0056	034	0132	079	0202	014	0269	008	0366	211
0057	034	0134	080	0205	014	0270	161	0367	211
0058	034	0136	080	0212	366	0272	161	0369	014
0060	034	0142	086	0213	018	0309	174	0370	014
0061	034	0145	086	0214	394	0310	174	0371	014
0068	036	0155	086	0215	020	0312	174	0374	357
0070	036	0156	087	0216	020	0314	174	0375	005
0076	038	0157	090	0217	020	0319	174	0376	021
0079	041	0158	090	0219	020	0322	174	0377	021
0080	041	0159	090	0220	020	0328	009	0380	021
0081	041	0160	090	0225	022	0329	180	0386	476
0082	042	0165	005	0226	022	0330	190	0389	234
0083	042	0166	100	0227	007	0332	196	0396	232

0398	232	0539	278	0637	017	0753	429	0906	026
0400	232	0541	278	0639	017	0759	431	0907	026
0402	232	0542	278	0640	356	0766	432	0908	026
0403	234	0543	278	0641	356	0776	436	0909	026
0404	237	0544	278	0642	356	0779	438	0910	026
0405	237	0545	278	0644	017	0781	439	0922	027
0406	240	0546	278	0645	093	0782	439	0923	031
0408	247	0547	278	0645	357	0784	021	0925	042
0410	012	0548	278	0646	356	0786	021	0926	034
0410	247	0551	278	0648	364	0793	444	0928	034
0411	012	0552	278	0650	371	0794	444	0929	035
0413	012	0553	282	0651	364	0800	021	0930	035
0421	012	0554	282	0652	364	0801	021	0931	036
0422	012	0555	282	0653	364	0803	021	0933	041
0423	012	0556	282	0655	366	0808	021	0934	042
0424	012	0559	284	0656	367	0809	021	0935	027
0427	012	0561	284	0657	367	0810	451	0936	029
0428	012	0562	284	0659	368	0815	452	0937	029
0430	012	0565	284	0660	368	0816	453	0939	029
0432	247	0570	285	0661	017	0817	453	0943	033
0433	012	0571	278	0662	371	0818	453	0944	034
0434	247	0577	291	0665	372	0819	453	0947	037
0436	012	0578	291	0668	372	0820	453	0948	040
0437	012	0579	291	0678	386	0825	457	0950	041
0444	250	0580	014	0679	386	0827	457	0952	240
0451	012	0584	294	0680	386	0830	457	0953	240
0457	247	0585	294	0681	386	0833	460	0954	043
0480	247	0587	014	0686	394	0834	460	0955	043
0481	255	0589	014	0689	019	0835	460	0957	029
0482	255	0590	014	0693	420	0836	460	0958	029
0483	255	0591	014	0695	420	0837	460	0959	029
0485	255	0592	291	0696	420	0838	460	0960	029
0488	255	0594	297	0697	420	0839	460	0961	029
0489	255	0595	014	0698	420	0842	460	0962	029
0490	255	0596	291	0699	420	0853	022	0963	029
0491	255	0597	301	0707	421	0854	022	0981	031
0492	255	0602	305	0708	421	0855	022	0994	027
0509	256	0603	305	0710	421	0857	022	0995	036
0517	013	0604	305	0713	421	0859	022	0996	036
0518	013	0610	319	0717	020	0860	476	0998	036
0519	013	0611	322	0723	020	0862	481	1000	040
0520	013	0612	328	0724	429	0866	476	1002	042
0523	013	0614	325	0727	020	0868	476	1004	044
0525	278	0615	328	0729	425	0872	027	1055	044
0527	101	0616	328	0730	425	0874	240	1057	033
0527	278	0618	321	0731	425	0875	240	1058	033
0528	278	0622	325	0732	426	0877	240	1059	033
0529	278	0624	325	0734	426	0887	043	1065	033
0530	278	0625	325	0736	426	0889	043	1068	033
0533	282	0626	325	0737	426	0890	043	1077	034
0534	284	0627	325	0738	423	0891	043	1086	034
0535	276	0628	325	0748	429	0892	024	1087	034
0536	276	0631	328	0750	429	0897	029	1089	034
0537	276	0632	328	0752	429	0905	026	1091	034

1094	034	1360	046	1531	056	1725	086	1824	079
1097	034	1361	046	1534	056	1726	086	1825	079
1098	034	1362	046	1536	056	1727	068	1826	079
1101	034	1363	046	1538	056	1728	069	1827	079
1115	034	1364	046	1540	342	1729	069	1843	082
1116	035	1365	046	1543	056	1730	070	1844	082
1119	035	1406	047	1544	056	1731	070	1847	082
1121	036	1407	048	1546	342	1733	070	1848	083
1129	036	1408	048	1549	056	1736	070	1851	085
1140	036	1409	048	1550	056	1738	071	1852	085
1143	036	1413	048	1552	056	1739	071	1854	085
1146	036	1415	048	1556	056	1740	074	1858	086
1158	038	1416	048	1557	056	1741	071	1860	086
1164	038	1417	048	1558	056	1742	071	1863	086
1206	040	1418	048	1561	056	1743	077	1865	086
1207	040	1423	048	1571	057	1745	079	1866	086
1228	041	1428	048	1572	057	1747	079	1876	087
1238	041	1429	048	1573	057	1748	079	1877	087
1248	042	1454	049	1588	058	1750	084	1881	088
1249	042	1455	049	1593	058	1752	086	1887	093
1250	042	1456	049	1594	058	1754	086	1889	093
1252	042	1457	064	1598	058	1755	086	1890	090
1253	042	1458	049	1600	060	1758	077	1891	034
1254	042	1460	049	1610	046	1760	074	1892	034
1257	042	1461	046	1615	064	1762	074	1895	042
1262	042	1462	046	1616	064	1767	071	1897	091
1267	042	1464	048	1620	064	1770	069	1898	091
1274	042	1465	049	1621	064	1771	069	1899	091
1277	042	1466	049	1624	064	1772	071	1900	091
1278	042	1468	051	1625	064	1773	071	1901	091
1279	042	1471	049	1626	064	1777	080	1902	091
1285	042	1472	049	1627	064	1779	080	1903	091
1287	042	1473	342	1628	064	1781	080	1906	092
1305	042	1478	060	1641	064	1785	077	1911	092
1322	043	1479	061	1659	065	1786	087	1915	077
1323	036	1480	061	1660	066	1788	087	1916	079
1324	044	1481	064	1669	068	1790	077	1917	079
1326	044	1482	064	1670	068	1792	077	1918	081
1327	044	1484	064	1671	068	1793	077	1920	083
1341	049	1487	065	1672	069	1794	077	1921	086
1342	049	1488	051	1674	069	1795	077	1925	086
1343	049	1491	051	1675	071	1796	077	1926	086
1344	049	1492	051	1676	071	1800	078	1927	086
1346	049	1494	051	1677	068	1802	078	1929	093
1347	049	1496	051	1679	068	1803	078	1930	093
1348	049	1503	051	1680	068	1805	078	1931	093
1349	049	1512	052	1681	068	1808	078	1931	093
1350	056	1516	049	1686	068	1809	078	1933	093
1351	056	1517	048	1709	069	1817	078	1933	093
1352	056	1518	052	1710	069	1818	079	1935	092
1353	056	1523	056	1711	069	1819	079	1942	093
1354	046	1524	056	1717	070	1820	079	1942	093
1356	046	1525	056	1718	070	1822	079	1943	093
1357	046	1530	056	1724	079	1823	079	1943	093

Appendix F – Strong's to Ancient Hebrew

1945 093	2029 108	2151 144	2356 240	2534 167
1947 100	2030 108	2154 145	2357 174	2535 167
1948 100	2032 108	2161 145	2363 175	2545 167
1949 101	2034 433	2162 145	2372 161	2552 167
1951 102	2035 433	2177 146	2373 161	2553 167
1952 102	2038 431	2181 146	2374 161	2573 167
1957 095	2040 433	2183 146	2377 161	2580 168
1958 093	2041 433	2184 146	2378 161	2583 168
1959 092	2042 108	2185 146	2380 161	2587 168
1960 092	2046 473	2188 148	2384 161	2588 168
1961 093	2048 474	2189 148	2385 161	2589 168
1962 093	2049 474	2203 149	2397 162	2594 168
1963 005	2050 110	2212 151	2398 163	2595 168
1964 232	2053 116	2213 152	2399 163	2600 168
1966 100	2054 152	2214 394	2400 163	2603 168
1969 102	2056 246	2219 152	2401 163	2620 169
1970 240	2061 134	2223 152	2403 163	2622 169
1971 240	2063 137	2237 152	2416 159	2643 171
1972 100	2070 310	2239 152	2420 158	2644 171
1973 100	2085 135	2243 156	2421 159	2645 171
1974 100	2086 136	2244 156	2422 159	2646 171
1975 249	2087 136	2245 156	2424 159	2653 171
1976 249	2088 137	2247 156	2425 159	2671 172
1977 249	2089 379	2253 156	2426 166	2673 172
1978 253	2090 137	2282 157	2427 166	2676 172
1979 253	2091 134	2283 157	2428 166	2677 172
1980 253	2092 145	2287 157	2430 166	2678 172
1982 253	2094 394	2288 157	2433 168	2686 172
1984 100	2096 394	2297 158	2434 172	2687 172
1986 255	2097 137	2299 158	2435 172	2706 173
1988 100	2098 137	2300 158	2436 173	2707 173
1991 101	2100 134	2302 158	2439 175	2708 173
1992 093	2101 134	2303 158	2440 175	2710 173
1992 101	2102 136	2304 158	2441 165	2711 173
1993 101	2106 137	2325 156	2442 165	2715 174
1995 101	2107 144	2326 156	2443 165	2716 174
1998 101	2108 144	2328 157	2455 166	2734 174
2000 101	2109 146	2329 157	2456 166	2740 174
2003 279	2111 148	2330 158	2457 166	2746 174
2004 093	2113 148	2331 159	2470 166	2750 174
2010 294	2114 394	2333 159	2471 166	2751 174
2013 103	2115 394	2336 162	2474 166	2787 174
2014 355	2116 394	2337 162	2479 166	2788 174
2015 363	2118 140	2339 163	2481 166	2814 175
2016 363	2121 136	2342 166	2483 166	2842 417
2017 363	2123 139	2344 166	2484 166	2844 176
2018 363	2131 151	2345 167	2485 166	2846 176
2019 363	2132 154	2346 167	2486 166	2847 176
2020 386	2134 143	2347 169	2490 166	2849 176
2021 388	2135 143	2348 171	2491 166	2851 176
2022 108	2137 143	2351 172	2524 167	2865 176
2026 421	2141 143	2352 240	2525 167	2866 176
2027 421	2149 144	2353 174	2527 167	2889 196
2028 421	2150 144	2355 174	2529 167	2890 196

2891	196	3010	046	3211	246	3314	368	3445	448
2892	196	3013	091	3212	253	3318	379	3447	449
2893	196	3014	091	3213	254	3320	376	3451	453
2894	181	3015	091	3214	254	3322	377	3452	453
2895	178	3016	064	3215	254	3323	394	3453	461
2896	178	3018	060	3216	258	3326	390	3455	453
2898	178	3019	060	3217	259	3329	379	3456	453
2901	181	3021	060	3218	239	3331	390	3462	454
2902	184	3022	060	3220	211	3332	393	3463	454
2903	193	3023	060	3222	211	3333	393	3465	454
2904	188	3024	060	3225	278	3334	394	3467	456
2905	196	3025	064	3227	278	3335	394	3468	456
2907	197	3027	202	3231	278	3336	394	3471	457
2909	184	3032	202	3233	278	3338	394	3474	460
2910	184	3033	070	3235	284	3341	396	3476	460
2911	184	3034	202	3237	285	3342	398	3477	460
2915	184	3039	070	3238	291	3344	400	3483	460
2916	185	3045	082	3240	294	3349	401	3486	461
2918	196	3049	082	3242	305	3350	400	3489	466
2919	188	3051	090	3243	305	3351	409	3490	475
2921	188	3053	090	3245	312	3352	417	3491	460
2922	188	3093	108	3246	312	3353	417	3498	460
2924	188	3095	255	3247	312	3357	416	3499	460
2925	188	3104	034	3248	312	3363	412	3502	482
2926	188	3105	034	3249	328	3364	414	3504	482
2930	189	3117	211	3250	328	3365	416	3508	482
2931	189	3119	211	3251	393	3366	416	3510	222
2932	189	3121	212	3254	325	3368	416	3511	222
2933	189	3123	212	3256	328	3369	417	3512	225
2935	190	3126	305	3257	214	3372	218	3518	222
2937	192	3127	305	3259	334	3373	218	3537	224
2945	193	3138	218	3261	214	3374	218	3539	224
2952	193	3148	482	3264	350	3381	422	3541	093
2961	196	3154	148	3267	337	3384	218	3541	225
2968	002	3161	158	3271	339	3387	437	3543	225
2969	005	3162	158	3276	342	3391	426	3544	225
2973	247	3173	158	3277	342	3394	426	3545	225
2974	012	3175	166	3280	342	3399	427	3547	234
2975	218	3176	166	3282	344	3401	420	3548	234
2976	021	3179	167	3283	344	3407	421	3550	234
2978	022	3182	171	3284	344	3409	429	3554	225
2980	200	3186	174	3286	347	3411	429	3555	225
2981	034	3187	169	3287	347	3415	421	3556	222
2986	034	3188	169	3288	347	3417	437	3557	232
2988	034	3190	178	3289	348	3418	437	3559	234
2990	034	3196	212	3293	350	3419	437	3561	234
2992	035	3197	202	3295	350	3420	437	3563	235
2993	035	3198	228	3302	357	3422	437	3564	240
2994	035	3201	232	3303	357	3423	439	3581	228
3001	043	3205	246	3304	357	3424	439	3587	225
3002	043	3206	246	3306	360	3425	439	3588	225
3004	043	3207	246	3307	360	3426	021	3589	224
3006	043	3208	246	3308	357	3427	442	3590	224
3009	046	3209	246	3313	368	3444	456	3591	224

Appendix F – Strong's to Ancient Hebrew

3595	240	3807	242	3971	277	4072	074	4157	349
3596	232	3808	247	3972	277	4078	071	4159	357
3599	235	3811	247	3973	279	4079	080	4160	282
3600	240	3813	251	3974	020	4082	080	4161	379
3602	093	3814	251	3975	020	4085	077	4163	379
3602	225	3816	255	3976	146	4090	080	4164	393
3605	232	3820	244	3978	232	4093	082	4165	393
3607	232	3823	244	3979	232	4098	087	4166	393
3608	232	3824	244	3980	232	4100	269	4167	283
3610	232	3826	244	3981	282	4102	269	4168	400
3615	232	3827	244	3982	284	4103	101	4169	400
3616	232	3833	244	3985	278	4106	284	4170	417
3617	232	3834	244	3986	278	4107	276	4171	284
3618	232	3849	245	3987	278	4108	253	4172	218
3623	232	3851	244	3988	279	4109	253	4173	421
3627	232	3852	244	3989	017	4110	100	4174	422
3628	232	3854	245	3990	364	4112	255	4175	218
3629	232	3856	247	3991	364	4113	284	4177	218
3631	232	3859	255	3992	284	4114	363	4178	427
3632	232	3862	408	3993	420	4115	363	4180	439
3634	232	3863	247	3994	438	4116	284	4181	439
3642	233	3867	247	3996	027	4117	284	4184	285
3644	234	3868	249	3997	027	4118	284	4185	285
3651	234	3869	249	3998	033	4119	284	4186	442
3653	234	3871	250	3999	034	4120	284	4190	456
3654	234	3874	251	4000	036	4123	474	4191	286
3655	234	3875	251	4001	037	4126	027	4192	286
3657	234	3880	247	4002	038	4127	267	4194	286
3661	234	3883	254	4003	041	4128	268	4195	482
3674	234	3884	254	4008	031	4129	082	4198	271
3676	235	3885	256	4011	036	4130	082	4200	271
3677	235	3886	258	4016	043	4131	273	4201	139
3678	235	3887	260	4032	064	4132	273	4202	146
3680	235	3888	264	4033	064	4133	273	4204	394
3681	235	3891	249	4034	064	4134	275	4205	394
3682	235	3892	250	4035	064	4135	276	4206	140
3699	235	3893	250	4039	056	4136	276	4209	145
3704	235	3895	250	4041	057	4138	246	4214	152
3709	237	3897	250	4042	058	4139	276	4215	152
3710	237	3909	251	4043	058	4141	310	4220	272
3711	237	3910	251	4044	058	4142	310	4221	272
3712	237	3911	251	4050	064	4142	310	4222	272
3721	237	3914	247	4055	268	4143	312	4224	156
3733	240	3915	254	4058	268	4144	312	4229	272
3734	240	3917	254	4059	268	4145	312	4230	157
3738	240	3918	264	4060	268	4146	312	4231	161
3739	240	3924	254	4062	134	4147	328	4234	166
3740	240	3930	258	4063	268	4148	328	4236	161
3741	240	3944	260	4064	071	4150	334	4237	161
3746	240	3945	260	4065	074	4151	334	4239	272
3753	240	3952	250	4066	080	4152	334	4241	159
3769	240	3966	004	4067	080	4154	334	4242	174
3780	235	3967	269	4069	082	4155	347	4245	166
3795	242	3970	005	4071	086	4156	348	4246	166

Ancient Hebrew Language and Alphabet

4247	166	4395	298	4561	328	4693	394	4828	421
4251	166	4396	298	4562	328	4694	394	4828	434
4260	167	4397	253	4568	332	4698	386	4829	434
4264	168	4399	253	4578	280	4699	386	4830	434
4268	169	4400	253	4579	280	4700	386	4832	435
4275	172	4402	298	4580	333	4702	390	4835	436
4276	172	4405	284	4581	337	4707	391	4843	284
4279	174	4407	298	4583	344	4711	282	4844	284
4280	174	4411	256	4585	344	4712	394	4845	284
4283	174	4412	256	4588	347	4716	283	4846	284
4288	176	4425	284	4589	350	4721	408	4855	307
4289	176	4426	260	4593	339	4723	401	4857	457
4291	273	4448	284	4594	339	4724	401	4858	301
4292	181	4461	268	4596	335	4725	409	4859	307
4294	273	4463	286	4598	342	4726	240	4859	307
4295	273	4470	284	4599	344	4727	404	4860	307
4296	273	4472	284	4605	342	4728	404	4860	307
4297	273	4478	269	4607	342	4731	408	4862	452
4298	273	4480	278	4608	342	4735	410	4863	460
4299	181	4482	278	4609	342	4736	410	4864	301
4300	188	4487	278	4611	342	4743	283	4870	443
4307	196	4488	278	4616	344	4744	416	4871	285
4310	269	4489	278	4617	344	4745	416	4874	307
4315	178	4490	278	4618	344	4746	416	4875	445
4323	232	4492	306	4624	349	4747	416	4876	445
4325	269	4493	290	4626	350	4748	417	4878	442
4327	278	4494	294	4629	350	4749	417	4879	443
4328	312	4496	294	4630	350	4750	417	4880	449
4329	319	4497	300	4631	350	4751	284	4881	319
4330	282	4498	301	4636	350	4752	284	4882	455
4334	460	4499	301	4639	345	4753	284	4884	328
4339	460	4500	306	4647	360	4754	284	4885	323
4340	460	4501	306	4650	370	4758	423	4889	448
4341	222	4503	294	4652	364	4759	423	4892	448
4348	225	4507	278	4660	370	4760	423	4895	304
4349	234	4512	298	4661	370	4761	439	4897	285
4350	234	4517	302	4671	282	4763	439	4906	319
4351	240	4518	305	4672	282	4766	420	4923	453
4355	275	4521	278	4673	376	4767	420	4932	454
4356	232	4522	279	4674	376	4768	420	4933	455
4357	232	4523	279	4675	376	4784	284	4935	456
4358	232	4524	310	4679	378	4786	284	4942	457
4359	232	4527	312	4680	282	4787	284	4943	459
4360	232	4529	279	4682	282	4788	422	4944	459
4361	232	4530	279	4683	304	4791	431	4945	459
4369	234	4531	301	4684	144	4793	436	4951	328
4371	235	4533	313	4685	378	4794	436	4952	460
4372	235	4534	319	4686	378	4805	284	4959	285
4374	235	4539	319	4687	379	4806	284	4960	462
4380	240	4540	319	4688	386	4808	420	4962	286
4390	298	4546	320	4689	393	4814	284	4963	036
4392	298	4547	320	4690	393	4815	284	4970	286
4393	298	4549	279	4691	393	4816	429	4974	475
4394	298	4554	325	4692	394	4820	431	4975	476

4984	301	5133	301	5433	310	5637	328	5810	337
4994	291	5134	305	5435	310	5638	330	5842	339
4995	291	5136	307	5437	310	5645	332	5844	339
4997	290	5137	293	5438	310	5646	332	5856	335
4998	291	5148	294	5439	310	5672	332	5860	339
4999	291	5168	014	5465	312	5692	333	5861	339
5000	291	5186	295	5469	328	5703	334	5868	343
5001	299	5204	291	5470	328	5704	334	5869	344
5002	299	5205	290	5472	311	5706	334	5879	344
5006	304	5206	290	5473	311	5707	334	5888	347
5007	304	5207	294	5475	312	5708	334	5889	347
5008	305	5209	300	5478	316	5710	334	5890	347
5009	305	5211	301	5479	317	5712	334	5892	350
5010	306	5214	306	5480	319	5713	334	5895	350
5012	288	5215	306	5483	323	5715	334	5920	342
5014	288	5216	306	5484	323	5716	334	5921	342
5016	288	5217	297	5486	325	5718	334	5923	342
5030	288	5218	297	5488	325	5719	334	5927	342
5031	288	5219	297	5490	325	5743	332	5929	342
5050	289	5221	297	5492	325	5746	333	5930	342
5051	289	5222	297	5493	328	5749	334	5932	342
5054	289	5223	297	5494	328	5750	334	5934	342
5058	289	5238	297	5496	330	5753	335	5940	342
5067	290	5239	298	5497	330	5754	335	5942	342
5074	290	5240	029	5500	316	5756	337	5944	342
5076	290	5251	301	5501	316	5763	342	5945	342
5077	290	5254	301	5509	311	5764	342	5948	342
5078	290	5255	301	5518	328	5765	342	5949	342
5079	290	5263	307	5519	319	5766	342	5950	342
5091	291	5264	301	5520	319	5767	342	5953	342
5092	291	5299	303	5521	319	5768	342	5955	342
5093	291	5316	303	5522	319	5770	344	5971	343
5101	305	5317	303	5526	319	5771	344	5973	343
5102	306	5323	301	5536	320	5772	344	5978	343
5104	306	5327	304	5537	320	5773	344	5980	343
5105	306	5352	305	5541	320	5774	347	6004	343
5106	291	5355	305	5542	320	5775	347	6030	344
5107	288	5356	305	5544	320	5779	348	6031	344
5108	288	5357	305	5549	320	5781	349	6035	344
5110	290	5377	307	5550	320	5782	350	6037	344
5112	290	5378	307	5551	320	5783	350	6038	344
5115	291	5379	307	5552	320	5785	350	6039	344
5116	291	5382	307	5561	453	5786	350	6040	344
5117	294	5383	307	5572	322	5787	350	6041	344
5118	294	5384	307	5577	322	5788	350	6045	344
5120	295	5385	307	5580	323	5789	175	6049	344
5123	299	5386	307	5584	324	5790	175	6051	344
5124	299	5388	307	5584	445	5791	352	6053	344
5125	300	5405	307	5592	325	5792	352	6071	345
5127	301	5406	307	5595	325	5794	337	6072	345
5128	302	5429	313	5605	325	5795	337	6073	347
5130	303	5430	322	5620	328	5797	337	6079	347
5131	303	5431	322	5627	328	5807	337	6086	348
5132	301	5432	313	5630	328	5808	337	6095	348

6096	348	6366	357	6654	378	6749	386	6961	401
6097	348	6368	360	6658	378	6750	386	6962	405
6098	348	6371	365	6660	378	6751	386	6963	408
6125	349	6374	357	6668	134	6752	386	6965	409
6145	350	6375	371	6669	134	6757	386	6967	409
6168	350	6378	363	6670	144	6767	386	6968	409
6169	350	6379	363	6671	394	6770	387	6969	410
6172	350	6381	364	6672	394	6771	387	6971	413
6176	350	6382	364	6673	379	6772	387	6972	414
6181	350	6383	364	6674	379	6773	387	6973	414
6185	350	6395	364	6675	379	6774	387	6974	414
6199	350	6414	364	6677	394	6777	387	6975	414
6209	350	6415	364	6679	378	6782	387	6977	414
6211	093	6416	364	6680	379	6791	388	6978	401
6211	351	6417	364	6681	382	6792	388	6979	240
6213	345	6419	364	6682	382	6793	388	6980	240
6244	351	6434	366	6683	386	6796	388	6982	240
6256	352	6435	366	6684	387	6803	388	6983	417
6258	352	6437	366	6685	387	6808	390	6985	405
6261	352	6438	366	6687	149	6816	390	6990	405
6284	357	6440	366	6688	149	6822	391	7006	401
6285	093	6443	366	6692	392	6823	391	7009	409
6285	357	6446	367	6693	393	6824	391	7012	409
6286	372	6451	367	6694	393	6826	391	7013	410
6287	372	6461	367	6695	393	6828	391	7015	410
6288	372	6463	368	6696	394	6830	391	7019	414
6289	372	6475	370	6697	394	6836	391	7020	414
6291	355	6499	372	6699	394	6844	391	7021	401
6299	356	6500	372	6702	396	6850	391	7022	408
6302	356	6501	372	6703	382	6851	391	7023	240
6304	356	6509	372	6704	382	6862	394	7031	408
6306	356	6510	372	6705	382	6864	394	7033	408
6310	357	6512	372	6706	382	6869	394	7034	408
6311	357	6517	372	6707	382	6872	394	7035	408
6313	355	6529	372	6708	382	6875	394	7036	408
6314	355	6565	372	6710	382	6887	394	7039	408
6315	360	6580	373	6716	379	6892	401	7043	408
6320	363	6581	373	6718	378	6893	401	7044	408
6321	364	6595	374	6719	378	6894	398	7045	408
6323	366	6596	374	6720	378	6895	398	7052	408
6327	370	6601	374	6723	382	6896	398	7054	409
6328	371	6612	374	6724	379	6897	398	7064	410
6329	371	6615	374	6725	379	6898	398	7065	410
6330	371	6626	374	6728	379	6915	400	7067	410
6331	372	6627	379	6731	392	6916	400	7068	410
6333	372	6629	379	6733	392	6936	400	7069	410
6335	373	6631	379	6734	392	6949	401	7070	410
6337	359	6632	376	6735	394	6950	408	7072	410
6338	359	6633	376	6736	394	6951	408	7075	410
6339	359	6635	376	6737	394	6952	408	7077	410
6341	360	6638	376	6738	386	6953	408	7082	414
6346	360	6639	376	6740	386	6957	401	7083	235
6351	360	6643	376	6742	386	6958	401	7085	412
6365	356	6646	376	6748	386	6960	401	7087	413

7093	414	7228	420	7388	438	7533	436	7705	444
7096	414	7230	420	7389	439	7541	437	7706	444
7097	414	7231	420	7390	429	7545	426	7709	312
7098	414	7232	420	7391	429	7550	437	7716	379
7099	414	7233	420	7401	429	7556	437	7717	312
7101	414	7235	420	7411	431	7558	439	7720	328
7112	414	7237	420	7413	431	7567	439	7721	313
7117	414	7239	420	7415	431	7568	439	7722	445
7119	416	7241	420	7416	431	7578	427	7723	445
7120	416	7286	422	7419	431	7579	457	7725	442
7121	416	7287	422	7423	431	7580	443	7726	442
7122	416	7289	422	7426	431	7581	443	7728	442
7124	416	7292	420	7427	431	7582	445	7729	442
7125	416	7293	420	7434	437	7583	445	7734	311
7135	416	7295	420	7435	437	7584	445	7735	311
7136	416	7296	420	7436	437	7585	452	7736	444
7137	416	7297	423	7438	432	7588	445	7737	445
7147	416	7298	427	7439	432	7589	449	7738	445
7148	416	7300	422	7440	432	7590	449	7742	448
7150	416	7301	423	7442	432	7591	445	7743	448
7151	416	7302	423	7443	432	7592	452	7745	448
7176	416	7304	426	7444	432	7596	452	7750	317
7179	417	7305	426	7445	432	7599	454	7751	449
7180	417	7306	426	7447	433	7600	454	7752	449
7184	235	7307	426	7450	433	7601	455	7753	319
7185	417	7309	426	7451	421	7602	457	7754	319
7186	417	7310	423	7452	434	7603	460	7757	452
7190	417	7311	431	7453	434	7604	460	7758	452
7193	411	7312	431	7454	434	7605	460	7760	321
7197	417	7315	431	7455	421	7607	460	7762	453
7198	417	7317	431	7462	434	7608	460	7768	456
7199	417	7318	431	7463	434	7611	460	7769	456
7200	423	7321	421	7464	434	7612	445	7771	456
7201	423	7322	435	7465	421	7613	313	7772	456
7202	423	7323	436	7468	434	7616	442	7773	456
7203	423	7324	437	7469	434	7617	442	7775	456
7207	423	7325	438	7471	434	7618	442	7779	457
7209	423	7326	439	7473	434	7622	442	7783	459
7210	423	7329	425	7474	434	7628	442	7784	459
7212	423	7330	425	7475	434	7632	442	7785	459
7213	431	7332	425	7489	434	7633	442	7786	328
7214	431	7333	425	7495	435	7675	442	7787	328
7215	431	7334	425	7496	435	7679	311	7788	460
7217	439	7347	426	7497	435	7683	443	7789	460
7218	439	7371	426	7499	435	7684	443	7790	460
7219	431	7374	427	7500	435	7685	311	7791	460
7219	439	7377	423	7503	435	7686	443	7794	460
7221	439	7378	420	7504	435	7689	311	7795	328
7222	439	7379	420	7510	435	7699	444	7795	460
7223	439	7381	426	7517	435	7700	444	7797	323
7224	439	7383	435	7518	436	7701	444	7807	448
7225	439	7385	437	7519	436	7702	312	7811	316
7226	439	7386	437	7521	436	7703	444	7812	448
7227	420	7387	437	7522	436	7704	312	7813	316

Ancient Hebrew Language and Alphabet

7816 448	8033 453	8326 460	8428 467	8538 475
7817 448	8034 453	8336 461	8431 166	8539 475
7822 448	8047 453	8337 461	8432 473	8541 475
7825 448	8064 453	8338 461	8433 228	8543 276
7845 448	8074 453	8341 461	8435 246	8544 278
7846 317	8076 453	8342 461	8437 254	8545 284
7847 317	8077 453	8345 461	8438 258	8546 286
7848 449	8078 453	8346 461	8442 478	8548 268
7850 449	8079 453	8354 462	8443 347	8549 475
7862 445	8127 454	8356 462	8444 379	8552 475
7863 313	8130 322	8357 462	8446 482	8557 279
7867 310	8132 454	8358 462	8447 482	8558 284
7869 310	8135 322	8359 462	8448 482	8560 284
7870 442	8136 454	8360 462	8449 482	8561 284
7871 442	8138 454	8371 462	8451 218	8563 284
7872 310	8141 454	8372 467	8452 482	8564 284
7873 311	8142 454	8373 464	8453 442	8565 476
7874 312	8144 454	8374 464	8455 470	8566 476
7875 312	8145 454	8375 464	8456 469	8567 476
7876 445	8146 322	8376 467	8457 146	8568 476
7878 316	8147 454	8377 467	8462 166	8569 291
7879 316	8148 454	8378 005	8463 166	8570 288
7880 316	8150 454	8379 467	8466 168	8571 297
7881 316	8153 454	8380 475	8467 168	8572 299
7882 448	8154 455	8381 012	8469 168	8573 303
7885 449	8155 455	8382 475	8473 174	8574 306
7890 454	8159 456	8383 014	8474 174	8577 476
7891 460	8173 456	8384 476	8478 470	8582 478
7892 460	8191 456	8385 291	8481 470	8584 334
7893 461	8192 457	8386 291	8482 470	8585 342
7896 462	8193 325	8388 482	8484 473	8586 342
7897 462	8194 457	8389 482	8486 278	8589 344
7898 462	8205 457	8392 027	8492 439	8591 478
7899 319	8207 457	8393 027	8495 483	8593 350
7900 319	8222 325	8394 036	8496 473	8595 478
7904 451	8242 327	8395 037	8497 473	8596 479
7905 319	8248 459	8397 034	8499 234	8597 372
7907 319	8249 459	8398 034	8500 473	8600 370
7918 451	8250 459	8399 034	8501 473	8601 017
7944 452	8264 459	8400 034	8502 232	8605 364
7945 452	8268 459	8401 036	8503 232	8608 479
7951 452	8269 328	8403 036	8504 232	8611 479
7952 452	8270 460	8409 064	8510 474	8615 401
7953 452	8280 328	8410 086	8511 474	8617 409
7956 452	8281 460	8414 467	8513 247	8618 409
7957 244	8282 328	8415 101	8514 244	8622 413
7958 320	8284 460	8416 100	8518 474	8635 420
7959 452	8285 460	8417 100	8519 256	8636 420
7961 452	8293 460	8418 253	8522 474	8641 431
7962 452	8302 460	8419 363	8524 474	8642 431
7987 452	8306 460	8420 467	8529 258	8643 421
7988 452	8307 460	8424 046	8534 474	8644 435
7997 452	8323 328	8426 202	8535 475	8645 425
7998 452	8324 460	8427 467	8537 475	8649 431

8650	432
8655	435
8658	439
8663	445
8666	442
8667	321
8668	456
8669	459
8670	460
8671	456
8672	456
8673	456

Ancient Hebrew Number - Strong's Number

002	0001	012	0355	020	0220	027	3996	034	2981
002	0003	012	0360	020	0717	027	3997	034	2986
002	0024	012	0361	020	0723	027	4126	034	2988
002	0178	012	0365	020	0727	027	8392	034	2990
002	0340	012	0410	020	3974	027	8393	034	3104
002	0341	012	0411	020	3975	029	0897	034	3105
002	0342	012	0413	021	0376	029	0936	034	3999
002	2968	012	0421	021	0377	029	0937	034	8397
004	0108	012	0422	021	0380	029	0939	034	8398
004	0181	012	0423	021	0784	029	0957	034	8399
004	0182	012	0424	021	0786	029	0958	034	8400
004	0343	012	0427	021	0800	029	0959	035	0929
004	3966	012	0428	021	0801	029	0960	035	0930
005	0165	012	0430	021	0803	029	0961	035	1116
005	0176	012	0433	021	0808	029	0962	035	1119
005	0183	012	0436	021	0809	029	0963	035	2992
005	0184	012	0437	021	2976	029	5240	035	2993
005	0185	012	0451	021	3426	030	0019	035	2994
005	0188	012	2974	022	0225	031	0923	036	0068
005	0190	012	8381	022	0226	031	0981	036	0070
005	0194	013	0517	022	0853	031	4008	036	0931
005	0199	013	0518	022	0854	033	0055	036	0995
005	0335	013	0519	022	0855	033	0943	036	0996
005	0336	013	0520	022	0857	033	1057	036	0998
005	0337	013	0523	022	0859	033	1058	036	1121
005	0338	014	0202	022	2978	033	1059	036	1129
005	0339	014	0205	024	0892	033	1065	036	1140
005	0344	014	0369	026	0006	033	1068	036	1143
005	0346	014	0370	026	0008	033	3998	036	1146
005	0349	014	0371	026	0009	034	0056	036	1323
005	0351	014	0580	026	0010	034	0057	036	4000
005	0375	014	0587	026	0011	034	0058	036	4011
005	1963	014	0589	026	0012	034	0060	036	4963
005	2969	014	0590	026	0013	034	0061	036	8394
005	3970	014	0591	026	0905	034	0180	036	8401
005	8378	014	0595	026	0906	034	0926	036	8403
007	0227	014	5168	026	0907	034	0928	037	0018
007	0233	014	8383	026	0908	034	0944	037	0947
008	0251	017	0637	026	0909	034	1077	037	4001
008	0253	017	0639	026	0910	034	1086	037	8395
008	0254	017	0644	027	0014	034	1087	038	0076
008	0255	017	0661	027	0015	034	1089	038	1158
008	0260	017	3989	027	0016	034	1091	038	1164
008	0264	017	8601	027	0017	034	1094	038	4002
008	0269	018	0213	027	0034	034	1097	040	0948
009	0328	019	0689	027	0035	034	1098	040	1000
012	0193	020	0215	027	0872	034	1101	040	1206
012	0352	020	0216	027	0922	034	1115	040	1207
012	0353	020	0217	027	0935	034	1891	041	0079
012	0354	020	0219	027	0994	034	1892	041	0080

Appendix F – Ancient Hebrew to Strong's

041	0081	046	1363	056	1351	064	1615	071	1772
041	0933	046	1364	056	1352	064	1616	071	1773
041	0950	046	1365	056	1353	064	1620	071	4064
041	1228	046	1461	056	1523	064	1621	071	4078
041	1238	046	1462	056	1524	064	1624	074	1740
041	4003	046	1610	056	1525	064	1625	074	1760
042	0046	046	3009	056	1530	064	1626	074	1762
042	0047	046	3010	056	1531	064	1627	074	4065
042	0082	046	8424	056	1534	064	1628	074	4072
042	0083	047	1406	056	1536	064	1641	077	1743
042	0084	048	0092	056	1538	064	3016	077	1758
042	0925	048	1407	056	1543	064	3025	077	1785
042	0934	048	1408	056	1544	064	4032	077	1790
042	1002	048	1409	056	1549	064	4033	077	1792
042	1248	048	1413	056	1550	064	4034	077	1793
042	1249	048	1415	056	1552	064	4035	077	1794
042	1250	048	1416	056	1556	064	4050	077	1795
042	1252	048	1417	056	1557	064	8409	077	1796
042	1253	048	1418	056	1558	065	1487	077	1915
042	1254	048	1423	056	1561	065	1659	077	4085
042	1257	048	1428	056	4039	066	1660	078	1800
042	1262	048	1429	057	0098	068	1669	078	1802
042	1267	048	1464	057	0099	068	1670	078	1803
042	1274	048	1517	057	0100	068	1671	078	1805
042	1277	049	1341	057	1571	068	1677	078	1808
042	1278	049	1342	057	1572	068	1679	078	1809
042	1279	049	1343	057	1573	068	1680	078	1817
042	1285	049	1344	057	4041	068	1681	079	0119
042	1287	049	1346	058	0101	068	1686	079	0120
042	1305	049	1347	058	1588	068	1727	079	0122
042	1895	049	1348	058	1593	069	1672	079	0124
043	0887	049	1349	058	1594	069	1674	079	0125
043	0889	049	1454	058	1598	069	1709	079	0127
043	0890	049	1455	058	4042	069	1710	079	0132
043	0891	049	1456	058	4043	069	1711	079	1724
043	0954	049	1458	058	4044	069	1728	079	1745
043	0955	049	1460	060	1478	069	1729	079	1747
043	1322	049	1465	060	1600	069	1770	079	1748
043	3001	049	1466	060	3018	069	1771	079	1818
043	3002	049	1471	060	3019	070	1717	079	1819
043	3004	049	1472	060	3021	070	1718	079	1820
043	3006	049	1516	060	3022	070	1730	079	1822
043	4016	051	0093	060	3023	070	1731	079	1823
044	1004	051	1468	060	3024	070	1733	079	1824
044	1055	051	1488	061	0102	070	1736	079	1825
044	1324	051	1491	061	1479	070	3033	079	1826
044	1326	051	1492	061	1480	070	3039	079	1827
044	1327	051	1494	064	0095	071	1675	079	1916
046	1354	051	1496	064	0103	071	1676	079	1917
046	1356	051	1503	064	0107	071	1738	080	0113
046	1357	052	1512	064	1457	071	1739	080	0134
046	1360	052	1518	064	1481	071	1741	080	0136
046	1361	056	0096	064	1482	071	1742	080	1777
046	1362	056	1350	064	1484	071	1767	080	1779

080	1781	090	3051	100	8416	144	2108	157	2287
080	4066	090	3053	100	8417	144	2149	157	2288
080	4067	091	1897	101	0527	144	2150	157	2328
080	4079	091	1898	101	1949	144	2151	157	2329
080	4082	091	1899	101	1991	144	4684	157	4230
080	4090	091	1900	101	1992	144	6670	158	0258
081	1918	091	1901	101	1993	145	2092	158	0259
082	1843	091	1902	101	1995	145	2154	158	2297
082	1844	091	1903	101	1998	145	2161	158	2299
082	1847	091	3013	101	2000	145	2162	158	2300
082	3045	091	3014	101	4103	145	4209	158	2302
082	3049	091	3015	101	8415	146	0238	158	2303
082	4069	092	1906	102	1951	146	0239	158	2304
082	4093	092	1911	102	1952	146	0240	158	2330
082	4129	092	1935	102	1969	146	0241	158	2420
082	4130	092	1959	103	2013	146	2109	158	3161
083	1848	092	1960	108	2022	146	2177	158	3162
083	1920	093	0645	108	2029	146	2181	158	3173
084	1750	093	1887	108	2030	146	2183	159	0262
085	1851	093	1889	108	2032	146	2184	159	2331
085	1852	093	1929	108	2042	146	2185	159	2333
085	1854	093	1930	108	3093	146	3976	159	2416
086	0117	093	1931	110	2050	146	4202	159	2421
086	0142	093	1931	116	2053	146	8457	159	2422
086	0145	093	1933	134	0231	148	2111	159	2424
086	0155	093	1933	134	2061	148	2113	159	2425
086	1725	093	1942	134	2091	148	2188	159	4241
086	1726	093	1942	134	2100	148	2189	161	0270
086	1752	093	1943	134	2101	148	3154	161	0272
086	1754	093	1943	134	4062	149	2203	161	2372
086	1755	093	1945	134	6668	149	6687	161	2373
086	1858	093	1958	134	6669	149	6688	161	2374
086	1860	093	1961	135	2085	151	0246	161	2377
086	1863	093	1962	136	2086	151	2131	161	2378
086	1865	093	1992	136	2087	151	2212	161	2380
086	1866	093	2004	136	2102	152	2054	161	2384
086	1921	093	3541	136	2121	152	2213	161	2385
086	1925	093	3602	137	2063	152	2219	161	4231
086	1926	093	6211	137	2088	152	2223	161	4236
086	1927	093	6285	137	2090	152	2237	161	4237
086	4071	095	1957	137	2097	152	2239	162	2336
086	8410	100	0166	137	2098	152	4214	162	2337
087	0156	100	0167	137	2106	152	4215	162	2397
087	1786	100	0168	139	2123	154	2132	163	2339
087	1788	100	0174	139	4201	156	2243	163	2398
087	1876	100	1947	140	2118	156	2244	163	2399
087	1877	100	1948	140	4206	156	2245	163	2400
087	4098	100	1966	143	2134	156	2247	163	2401
088	1881	100	1972	143	2135	156	2253	163	2403
090	0157	100	1973	143	2137	156	2325	165	2441
090	0158	100	1974	143	2141	156	2326	165	2442
090	0159	100	1984	144	0235	156	4224	165	2443
090	0160	100	1988	144	0237	157	2282	166	2342
090	1890	100	4110	144	2107	157	2283	166	2344

166	2426	168	8467	174	4279	196	0332	225	3554
166	2427	168	8469	174	4280	196	0334	225	3555
166	2428	169	2347	174	4283	196	2889	225	3587
166	2430	169	2620	174	8473	196	2890	225	3588
166	2455	169	2622	174	8474	196	2891	225	3602
166	2456	169	3187	175	2363	196	2892	225	4348
166	2457	169	3188	175	2439	196	2893	228	3198
166	2470	169	4268	175	2440	196	2905	228	3581
166	2471	171	2348	175	2814	196	2918	228	8433
166	2474	171	2643	175	5789	196	2961	232	0396
166	2479	171	2644	175	5790	196	4307	232	0398
166	2481	171	2645	176	2844	197	2907	232	0400
166	2483	171	2646	176	2846	200	2980	232	0402
166	2484	171	2653	176	2847	202	3027	232	1964
166	2485	171	3182	176	2849	202	3032	232	3201
166	2486	172	2351	176	2851	202	3034	232	3557
166	2490	172	2434	176	2865	202	3197	232	3596
166	2491	172	2435	176	2866	202	8426	232	3605
166	3175	172	2671	176	4288	211	0366	232	3607
166	3176	172	2673	176	4289	211	0367	232	3608
166	4234	172	2676	178	2895	211	3117	232	3610
166	4245	172	2677	178	2896	211	3119	232	3615
166	4246	172	2678	178	2898	211	3220	232	3616
166	4247	172	2686	178	3190	211	3222	232	3617
166	4251	172	2687	178	4315	212	3121	232	3618
166	8431	172	4275	180	0329	212	3123	232	3623
166	8462	172	4276	181	2894	212	3196	232	3627
166	8463	173	2436	181	2901	214	3257	232	3628
167	2345	173	2706	181	4292	214	3261	232	3629
167	2346	173	2707	181	4299	218	2975	232	3631
167	2524	173	2708	184	2902	218	3138	232	3632
167	2525	173	2710	184	2909	218	3372	232	3634
167	2527	173	2711	184	2910	218	3373	232	3978
167	2529	174	0268	184	2911	218	3374	232	3979
167	2534	174	0309	184	2915	218	3384	232	3980
167	2535	174	0310	185	2916	218	4172	232	4323
167	2545	174	0312	188	2904	218	4175	232	4356
167	2552	174	0314	188	2919	218	4177	232	4357
167	2553	174	0319	188	2921	218	8451	232	4358
167	2573	174	0322	188	2922	222	3510	232	4359
167	3179	174	2353	188	2924	222	3511	232	4360
167	4260	174	2355	188	2925	222	3518	232	4361
168	2433	174	2357	188	2926	222	3556	232	8502
168	2580	174	2715	188	4300	222	4341	232	8503
168	2583	174	2716	189	2930	224	3537	232	8504
168	2587	174	2734	189	2931	224	3539	233	3642
168	2588	174	2740	189	2932	224	3589	234	0389
168	2589	174	2746	189	2933	224	3590	234	0403
168	2594	174	2750	190	0330	224	3591	234	3547
168	2595	174	2751	190	2935	225	3512	234	3548
168	2600	174	2787	192	2937	225	3541	234	3550
168	2603	174	2788	193	2903	225	3543	234	3559
168	4264	174	3186	193	2945	225	3544	234	3561
168	8466	174	4242	193	2952	225	3545	234	3644

234 3651	240 3746	249 1977	256 0509	276 4135
234 3653	240 3753	249 3868	256 3885	276 4136
234 3654	240 3769	249 3869	256 4411	276 4139
234 3655	240 4351	249 3891	256 4412	276 8543
234 3657	240 4380	250 0444	256 8519	277 3971
234 3661	240 4726	250 3871	258 3216	277 3972
234 3674	240 6979	250 3892	258 3886	278 0525
234 4349	240 6980	250 3893	258 3930	278 0527
234 4350	240 6982	250 3895	258 8438	278 0528
234 4369	240 7023	250 3897	258 8529	278 0529
234 8499	242 3795	250 3952	259 3217	278 0530
235 3563	242 3807	251 3813	260 3887	278 0539
235 3599	244 3820	251 3814	260 3944	278 0541
235 3676	244 3823	251 3874	260 3945	278 0542
235 3677	244 3824	251 3875	260 4426	278 0543
235 3678	244 3826	251 3909	264 3888	278 0544
235 3680	244 3827	251 3910	264 3918	278 0545
235 3681	244 3833	251 3911	267 4127	278 0546
235 3682	244 3834	253 1978	268 4055	278 0547
235 3699	244 3851	253 1979	268 4058	278 0548
235 3704	244 3852	253 1980	268 4059	278 0551
235 3780	244 7957	253 1982	268 4060	278 0552
235 4371	244 8514	253 3212	268 4063	278 0571
235 4372	245 3849	253 4108	268 4128	278 3225
235 4374	245 3854	253 4109	268 4461	278 3227
235 7083	246 2056	253 4397	268 8548	278 3231
235 7184	246 3205	253 4399	269 3967	278 3233
237 0404	246 3206	253 4400	269 4100	278 3985
237 0405	246 3207	253 8418	269 4102	278 3986
237 3709	246 3208	254 3213	269 4310	278 3987
237 3710	246 3209	254 3214	269 4325	278 4327
237 3711	246 3211	254 3215	269 4478	278 4480
237 3712	246 4138	254 3883	271 4198	278 4482
237 3721	246 8435	254 3884	271 4200	278 4487
239 3218	247 0191	254 3915	272 4220	278 4488
240 0406	247 0196	254 3917	272 4221	278 4489
240 0874	247 0200	254 3924	272 4222	278 4490
240 0875	247 0408	254 8437	272 4229	278 4507
240 0877	247 0410	255 0197	272 4239	278 4521
240 0952	247 0432	255 0199	273 4131	278 8486
240 0953	247 0434	255 0481	273 4132	278 8544
240 1970	247 0457	255 0482	273 4133	279 2003
240 1971	247 0480	255 0483	273 4291	279 3973
240 2352	247 2973	255 0485	273 4294	279 3988
240 2356	247 3808	255 0488	273 4295	279 4522
240 3564	247 3811	255 0489	273 4296	279 4523
240 3595	247 3856	255 0490	273 4297	279 4529
240 3600	247 3863	255 0491	273 4298	279 4530
240 3733	247 3867	255 0492	275 4134	279 4549
240 3734	247 3880	255 1986	275 4355	279 8557
240 3738	247 3914	255 3095	276 0535	280 4578
240 3739	247 8513	255 3816	276 0536	280 4579
240 3740	249 1975	255 3859	276 0537	282 0533
240 3741	249 1976	255 4112	276 4107	282 0553

282	0554	284	8563	291	5106	301	4984	307	4860
282	0555	284	8564	291	5115	301	5127	307	4874
282	0556	285	0570	291	5116	301	5132	307	5136
282	3981	285	3237	291	5204	301	5133	307	5263
282	4160	285	4184	291	8385	301	5211	307	5377
282	4330	285	4185	291	8386	301	5251	307	5378
282	4671	285	4871	291	8569	301	5254	307	5379
282	4672	285	4897	293	5137	301	5255	307	5382
282	4680	285	4959	294	0584	301	5264	307	5383
282	4682	286	4191	294	0585	301	5323	307	5384
282	4711	286	4192	294	2010	302	4517	307	5385
283	4167	286	4194	294	3240	302	5128	307	5386
283	4716	286	4463	294	4494	303	5130	307	5388
283	4743	286	4962	294	4496	303	5131	307	5405
284	0534	286	4970	294	4503	303	5299	307	5406
284	0559	286	8546	294	5117	303	5316	310	2070
284	0561	288	5012	294	5118	303	5317	310	4141
284	0562	288	5014	294	5148	303	8573	310	4142
284	0565	288	5016	294	5207	304	4683	310	4142
284	3235	288	5030	295	5120	304	4895	310	4524
284	3982	288	5031	295	5186	304	5006	310	5433
284	3992	288	5107	297	0594	304	5007	310	5435
284	4106	288	5108	297	5217	304	5327	310	5437
284	4113	288	8570	297	5218	305	0602	310	5438
284	4116	289	5050	297	5219	305	0603	310	5439
284	4117	289	5051	297	5221	305	0604	310	7867
284	4118	289	5054	297	5222	305	3126	310	7869
284	4119	289	5058	297	5223	305	3127	310	7872
284	4120	290	4493	297	5238	305	3242	311	5472
284	4171	290	4997	297	8571	305	3243	311	5473
284	4405	290	5067	298	4390	305	4518	311	5509
284	4425	290	5074	298	4392	305	5008	311	7679
284	4448	290	5076	298	4393	305	5009	311	7685
284	4470	290	5077	298	4394	305	5101	311	7689
284	4472	290	5078	298	4395	305	5134	311	7734
284	4751	290	5079	298	4396	305	5352	311	7735
284	4752	290	5110	298	4402	305	5355	311	7873
284	4753	290	5112	298	4407	305	5356	312	3245
284	4754	290	5205	298	4512	305	5357	312	3246
284	4784	290	5206	298	5239	306	4492	312	3247
284	4786	291	0577	299	5001	306	4500	312	3248
284	4787	291	0578	299	5002	306	4501	312	4143
284	4805	291	0579	299	5123	306	5010	312	4144
284	4806	291	0592	299	5124	306	5102	312	4145
284	4814	291	0596	299	8572	306	5104	312	4146
284	4815	291	3238	300	4497	306	5105	312	4328
284	4843	291	4994	300	5125	306	5214	312	4527
284	4844	291	4995	300	5209	306	5215	312	5465
284	4845	291	4998	301	0597	306	5216	312	5475
284	4846	291	4999	301	4498	306	8574	312	7702
284	8545	291	5000	301	4499	307	4855	312	7704
284	8558	291	5091	301	4531	307	4859	312	7709
284	8560	291	5092	301	4858	307	4859	312	7717
284	8561	291	5093	301	4864	307	4860	312	7874

312	7875	322	0611	328	5630	339	3271	344	4585
313	4533	322	5430	328	5637	339	4593	344	4599
313	5429	322	5431	328	7720	339	4594	344	4616
313	5432	322	5572	328	7786	339	5842	344	4617
313	7613	322	5577	328	7787	339	5844	344	4618
313	7721	322	8130	328	7795	339	5860	344	5770
313	7863	322	8135	328	8269	339	5861	344	5771
316	5478	322	8146	328	8280	342	1473	344	5772
316	5500	323	4885	328	8282	342	1540	344	5773
316	5501	323	5483	328	8323	342	1546	344	5869
316	7811	323	5484	330	5496	342	3276	344	5879
316	7813	323	5580	330	5497	342	3277	344	6030
316	7878	323	7797	330	5638	342	3280	344	6031
316	7879	324	5584	332	4568	342	4598	344	6035
316	7880	325	0614	332	5645	342	4605	344	6037
316	7881	325	0622	332	5646	342	4607	344	6038
317	5479	325	0624	332	5672	342	4608	344	6039
317	7750	325	0625	332	5743	342	4609	344	6040
317	7846	325	0626	333	4580	342	4611	344	6041
317	7847	325	0627	333	5692	342	5763	344	6045
319	0610	325	0628	333	5746	342	5764	344	6049
319	4329	325	3254	334	3259	342	5765	344	6051
319	4534	325	4554	334	4150	342	5766	344	6053
319	4539	325	5486	334	4151	342	5767	344	8589
319	4540	325	5488	334	4152	342	5768	345	4639
319	4881	325	5490	334	4154	342	5920	345	6071
319	4906	325	5492	334	5703	342	5921	345	6072
319	5480	325	5592	334	5704	342	5923	345	6213
319	5519	325	5595	334	5706	342	5927	347	3286
319	5520	325	5605	334	5707	342	5929	347	3287
319	5521	325	8193	334	5708	342	5930	347	3288
319	5522	325	8222	334	5710	342	5932	347	4155
319	5526	327	8242	334	5712	342	5934	347	4588
319	7753	328	0612	334	5713	342	5940	347	5774
319	7754	328	0615	334	5715	342	5942	347	5775
319	7899	328	0616	334	5716	342	5944	347	5888
319	7900	328	0631	334	5718	342	5945	347	5889
319	7905	328	0632	334	5719	342	5948	347	5890
319	7907	328	3249	334	5749	342	5949	347	6073
320	4546	328	3250	334	5750	342	5950	347	6079
320	4547	328	3256	334	8584	342	5953	347	8443
320	5536	328	4147	335	4596	342	5955	348	3289
320	5537	328	4148	335	5753	342	8585	348	4156
320	5541	328	4561	335	5754	342	8586	348	5779
320	5542	328	4562	335	5856	343	5868	348	6086
320	5544	328	4884	337	3267	343	5971	348	6095
320	5549	328	4951	337	4581	343	5973	348	6096
320	5550	328	5469	337	5756	343	5978	348	6097
320	5551	328	5470	337	5794	343	5980	348	6098
320	5552	328	5493	337	5795	343	6004	349	4157
320	7958	328	5494	337	5797	344	3282	349	4624
321	0618	328	5518	337	5807	344	3283	349	5781
321	7760	328	5620	337	5808	344	3284	349	6125
321	8667	328	5627	337	5810	344	4583	350	3264

350 3293	357 6285	366 6443	376 6632	386 4699
350 3295	357 6310	367 0656	376 6633	386 4700
350 4589	357 6311	367 0657	376 6635	386 6683
350 4626	357 6366	367 6446	376 6638	386 6738
350 4629	357 6374	367 6451	376 6639	386 6740
350 4630	359 6337	367 6461	376 6643	386 6742
350 4631	359 6338	368 0659	376 6646	386 6748
350 4636	359 6339	368 0660	377 3322	386 6749
350 5782	360 3306	368 3313	378 4679	386 6750
350 5783	360 3307	368 3314	378 4685	386 6751
350 5785	360 4647	368 6463	378 4686	386 6752
350 5786	360 6315	370 4650	378 6654	386 6757
350 5787	360 6341	370 4660	378 6658	386 6767
350 5788	360 6346	370 4661	378 6660	387 6684
350 5892	360 6351	370 6327	378 6679	387 6685
350 5895	360 6368	370 6475	378 6718	387 6770
350 6145	363 2015	370 8600	378 6719	387 6771
350 6168	363 2016	371 0650	378 6720	387 6772
350 6169	363 2017	371 0662	379 2089	387 6773
350 6172	363 2018	371 6328	379 3318	387 6774
350 6176	363 2019	371 6329	379 3329	387 6777
350 6181	363 4114	371 6330	379 4161	387 6782
350 6185	363 4115	371 6375	379 4163	388 2021
350 6199	363 6320	372 0665	379 4687	388 6791
350 6209	363 6378	372 0668	379 6627	388 6792
350 8593	363 6379	372 6286	379 6629	388 6793
351 6211	363 8419	372 6287	379 6631	388 6796
351 6244	364 0648	372 6288	379 6673	388 6803
352 5791	364 0651	372 6289	379 6674	390 3326
352 5792	364 0652	372 6331	379 6675	390 3331
352 6256	364 0653	372 6333	379 6680	390 4702
352 6258	364 3990	372 6499	379 6716	390 6808
352 6261	364 3991	372 6500	379 6724	390 6816
355 2014	364 4652	372 6501	379 6725	391 4707
355 6291	364 6321	372 6509	379 6728	391 6822
355 6313	364 6381	372 6510	379 7716	391 6823
355 6314	364 6382	372 6512	379 8444	391 6824
356 0640	364 6383	372 6517	382 6681	391 6826
356 0641	364 6395	372 6529	382 6682	391 6828
356 0642	364 6414	372 6565	382 6703	391 6830
356 0646	364 6415	372 8597	382 6704	391 6836
356 6299	364 6416	373 6335	382 6705	391 6844
356 6302	364 6417	373 6580	382 6706	391 6850
356 6304	364 6419	373 6581	382 6707	391 6851
356 6306	364 8605	374 6595	382 6708	392 6692
356 6365	365 6371	374 6596	382 6710	392 6731
357 0374	366 0212	374 6601	382 6723	392 6733
357 0645	366 0655	374 6612	386 0678	392 6734
357 3302	366 6323	374 6615	386 0679	393 3251
357 3303	366 6434	374 6626	386 0680	393 3332
357 3304	366 6435	376 3320	386 0681	393 3333
357 3308	366 6437	376 4673	386 2020	393 4164
357 4159	366 6438	376 4674	386 4688	393 4165
357 6284	366 6440	376 4675	386 4698	393 4166

393 4689	400 6915	410 7013	416 7151	421 2027
393 4690	400 6916	410 7015	416 7176	421 2028
393 4691	400 6936	410 7064	417 2842	421 3407
393 6693	401 3349	410 7065	417 3352	421 3415
393 6694	401 4723	410 7067	417 3353	421 4173
393 6695	401 4724	410 7068	417 3369	421 4828
394 0214	401 6892	410 7069	417 4170	421 7321
394 0232	401 6893	410 7070	417 4748	421 7451
394 0247	401 6949	410 7072	417 4749	421 7455
394 0686	401 6957	410 7075	417 4750	421 7465
394 2094	401 6958	410 7077	417 6983	421 8643
394 2096	401 6960	411 7193	417 7179	422 3381
394 2114	401 6961	412 3363	417 7180	422 4174
394 2115	401 6978	412 7085	417 7185	422 4788
394 2116	401 7006	413 6971	417 7186	422 7286
394 2214	401 7021	413 7087	417 7190	422 7287
394 3323	401 8615	413 8622	417 7197	422 7289
394 3334	404 4727	414 3364	417 7198	422 7300
394 3335	404 4728	414 6972	417 7199	423 0738
394 3336	405 6962	414 6973	420 0693	423 4758
394 3338	405 6985	414 6974	420 0695	423 4759
394 4204	405 6990	414 6975	420 0696	423 4760
394 4205	408 3862	414 6977	420 0697	423 7200
394 4692	408 4721	414 7019	420 0698	423 7201
394 4693	408 4731	414 7020	420 0699	423 7202
394 4694	408 6950	414 7082	420 3401	423 7203
394 4712	408 6951	414 7093	420 3993	423 7207
394 6671	408 6952	414 7096	420 4766	423 7209
394 6672	408 6953	414 7097	420 4767	423 7210
394 6677	408 6963	414 7098	420 4768	423 7212
394 6696	408 7022	414 7099	420 4808	423 7297
394 6697	408 7031	414 7101	420 7227	423 7301
394 6699	408 7033	414 7112	420 7228	423 7302
394 6735	408 7034	414 7117	420 7230	423 7310
394 6736	408 7035	416 3357	420 7231	423 7377
394 6737	408 7036	416 3365	420 7232	425 0729
394 6862	408 7039	416 3366	420 7233	425 0730
394 6864	408 7043	416 3368	420 7235	425 0731
394 6869	408 7044	416 4744	420 7237	425 7329
394 6872	408 7045	416 4745	420 7239	425 7330
394 6875	408 7052	416 4746	420 7241	425 7332
394 6887	409 3351	416 4747	420 7292	425 7333
396 3341	409 4725	416 7119	420 7293	425 7334
396 6702	409 6965	416 7120	420 7295	425 8645
398 3342	409 6967	416 7121	420 7296	426 0732
398 6894	409 6968	416 7122	420 7378	426 0734
398 6895	409 7009	416 7124	420 7379	426 0736
398 6896	409 7012	416 7125	420 8635	426 0737
398 6897	409 7054	416 7135	420 8636	426 3391
398 6898	409 8617	416 7136	421 0707	426 3394
400 3344	409 8618	416 7137	421 0708	426 7304
400 3350	410 4735	416 7147	421 0710	426 7305
400 4168	410 4736	416 7148	421 0713	426 7306
400 4169	410 6969	416 7150	421 2026	426 7307

426	7309	433	2034	437	7386	442	8453	449	7848
426	7347	433	2035	437	7387	442	8666	449	7850
426	7371	433	2040	437	7434	443	4870	449	7885
426	7381	433	2041	437	7435	443	4879	451	0810
426	7545	433	7447	437	7436	443	7580	451	7904
427	3399	433	7450	437	7541	443	7581	451	7918
427	4178	434	4828	437	7550	443	7683	452	0815
427	7298	434	4829	437	7556	443	7684	452	4862
427	7374	434	4830	438	0779	443	7686	452	7585
427	7578	434	7452	438	3994	444	0793	452	7592
429	0724	434	7453	438	7325	444	0794	452	7596
429	0748	434	7454	438	7388	444	7699	452	7757
429	0750	434	7462	439	0781	444	7700	452	7758
429	0752	434	7463	439	0782	444	7701	452	7944
429	0753	434	7464	439	3423	444	7703	452	7945
429	3409	434	7468	439	3424	444	7705	452	7951
429	3411	434	7469	439	3425	444	7706	452	7952
429	4816	434	7471	439	4180	444	7736	452	7953
429	7390	434	7473	439	4181	445	4875	452	7956
429	7391	434	7474	439	4761	445	4876	452	7959
429	7401	434	7475	439	4763	445	5584	452	7961
431	0759	434	7489	439	7217	445	7582	452	7962
431	2038	435	4832	439	7218	445	7583	452	7987
431	4791	435	7322	439	7219	445	7584	452	7988
431	4820	435	7383	439	7221	445	7588	452	7997
431	7213	435	7495	439	7222	445	7591	452	7998
431	7214	435	7496	439	7223	445	7612	453	0816
431	7215	435	7497	439	7224	445	7722	453	0817
431	7219	435	7499	439	7225	445	7723	453	0818
431	7311	435	7500	439	7226	445	7737	453	0819
431	7312	435	7503	439	7326	445	7738	453	0820
431	7315	435	7504	439	7389	445	7862	453	3451
431	7317	435	7510	439	7558	445	7876	453	3452
431	7318	435	7517	439	7567	445	8663	453	3455
431	7411	435	8644	439	7568	448	3445	453	3456
431	7413	435	8655	439	8492	448	4889	453	4923
431	7415	436	0776	439	8658	448	4892	453	5561
431	7416	436	4793	442	3427	448	7742	453	7762
431	7419	436	4794	442	4186	448	7743	453	8033
431	7423	436	4835	442	4878	448	7745	453	8034
431	7426	436	7323	442	7616	448	7807	453	8047
431	7427	436	7518	442	7617	448	7812	453	8064
431	8641	436	7519	442	7618	448	7816	453	8074
431	8642	436	7521	442	7622	448	7817	453	8076
431	8649	436	7522	442	7628	448	7822	453	8077
432	0766	436	7533	442	7632	448	7825	453	8078
432	7438	437	3387	442	7633	448	7845	453	8079
432	7439	437	3417	442	7675	448	7882	454	3462
432	7440	437	3418	442	7725	449	3447	454	3463
432	7442	437	3419	442	7726	449	4880	454	3465
432	7443	437	3420	442	7728	449	7589	454	4932
432	7444	437	3422	442	7729	449	7590	454	7599
432	7445	437	7324	442	7870	449	7751	454	7600
432	8650	437	7385	442	7871	449	7752	454	7890

205

454	8127	459	8248	461	8336	475	8382
454	8132	459	8249	461	8337	475	8535
454	8136	459	8250	461	8338	475	8537
454	8138	459	8264	461	8341	475	8538
454	8141	459	8268	461	8342	475	8539
454	8142	459	8669	461	8345	475	8541
454	8144	460	0833	461	8346	475	8549
454	8145	460	0834	462	4960	475	8552
454	8147	460	0835	462	7896	476	0386
454	8148	460	0836	462	7897	476	0860
454	8150	460	0837	462	7898	476	0866
454	8153	460	0838	462	8354	476	0868
455	4882	460	0839	462	8356	476	4975
455	4933	460	0842	462	8357	476	8384
455	7601	460	3474	462	8358	476	8565
455	8154	460	3476	462	8359	476	8566
455	8155	460	3477	462	8360	476	8567
456	3444	460	3483	462	8371	476	8568
456	3467	460	3491	464	8373	476	8577
456	3468	460	3498	464	8374	478	8442
456	4190	460	3499	464	8375	478	8582
456	4935	460	4334	466	3489	478	8591
456	7768	460	4339	467	8372	478	8595
456	7769	460	4340	467	8376	479	8596
456	7771	460	4863	467	8377	479	8608
456	7772	460	4952	467	8379	479	8611
456	7773	460	7603	467	8414	481	0862
456	7775	460	7604	467	8420	482	3148
456	8159	460	7605	467	8427	482	3502
456	8173	460	7607	467	8428	482	3504
456	8191	460	7608	469	8456	482	3508
456	8668	460	7611	470	8455	482	4195
456	8671	460	7788	470	8478	482	8388
456	8672	460	7789	470	8481	482	8389
456	8673	460	7790	470	8482	482	8446
457	0825	460	7791	473	2046	482	8447
457	0827	460	7794	473	8432	482	8448
457	0830	460	7795	473	8484	482	8449
457	3471	460	7891	473	8496	482	8452
457	4857	460	7892	473	8497	483	8495
457	4942	460	8270	473	8500		
457	7579	460	8281	473	8501		
457	7602	460	8284	474	2048		
457	7779	460	8285	474	2049		
457	8192	460	8293	474	4123		
457	8194	460	8302	474	8510		
457	8205	460	8306	474	8511		
457	8207	460	8307	474	8518		
459	4943	460	8324	474	8522		
459	4944	460	8326	474	8524		
459	4945	460	8670	474	8534		
459	7783	461	3453	475	3490		
459	7784	461	3486	475	4974		
459	7785	461	7893	475	8380		

Bibliography

Ancient Alphabets and Inscriptions

- "Writing," Smith's Bible Dictionary, 1987 ed.: 327.
- "Alphabet," The New Westminster Dictionary of the Bible, 1976 ed.: 30.
- "Writing," NIV Compact Dictionary of the Bible, 1989 ed.: 632-3.
- "Archeology and the Bible," The Lion Encyclopedia of the Bible, 1986 ed.: 38.
- "Writing," The New Harper's Bible Dictionary, 1973 ed.: 829.
- E. Raymond Capt, Missing Links Discovered in Assyrian Tablets (Thousand Oaks, Ca.: Artisan Sales, 1985) 24, 44.
- Ernst Doblhofer, Voices in Stone (New York, Viking Press, 1961) 35
- Frank Seekins, The Ten Commandments (Phoenix, Az.: Living Word Pictures, 1997)
- Emily Vermeule, Greece in the Bronze Age (Chicago, Ill. The University of Chicago Press, 1964)
- E.A. Wallis Budge The Book of the Dead (Secaucus, N.J. University Books, Inc. 1960)

Hebrew Culture

- William Smith, Smith's Bible Dictionary (Grand Rapids, Mi.: Zondervan, 1948)
- J.I. Packer, Merril C. Tenney, William White, Jr., Nelson's Illustrated Encyclopedia of Bible Facts (Nashville: Thomas Nelson, 1995) Madelene S. Miller

and J. Lane Miller, <u>Harper's Bible Dictionary</u>, (New York, Harper, 1973)

- Merrill F. Unger, <u>Unger's Bible Dictionary</u>, (Chicago, Moody, 1977)
- Henry H. Halley, <u>Halley's Bible Handbook</u> (Grand Rapids, Mi: Zondervan, 24th)
- <u>The New Westminster Dictionary of the Bible</u> (Philadelphia, Westminster, 1976)
- <u>NIV Compact Dictionary of the Bible</u>, (Grand Rapids, Zondervan, 1989)
- <u>The Lion Encyclopedia of the Bible</u>, (Tring England, Lion, new rev. ed.1986)
- Fred H. Wright, <u>Manners and Customs of Bible Lands</u> (Chicago: Moody, 1983)
- Madeleine S. Miller and J. Lane Miller, <u>Encyclopedia of Bible Life</u> (New York: Harper & Brothers, 1944)
- <u>Holman Bible Dictionary</u>, (Nashville, Holman, 1991)
- Mary Ellen Chase, <u>Life and Language in the Old Testament</u> (N.Y., W. W. Norton and Company Inc. 1955)
- Emmanuel Anati, <u>Palestine before the Hebrews</u> (N.Y., Alfred A. Knopf, 1963)
- Donald Powell Cole, <u>Nomads of the Nomads</u>, (Arlington Heights, Ill., Harlan Davidson, Inc., 1975)
- E. W. Heaton, <u>Everyday life in Old Testament times</u>, (New York, Charles Scribners, 1956)

Word Studies

- James Strong, <u>New Strong's Concise Dictionary of the Words in the Hebrew Bible</u>, (Nashville, Nelson, 1995)
- W. E. Vine, Merrill F. Unger, William White, <u>Vine's Expository Dictionary of Biblical Words</u>, (Nashville, Nelson, 1985)
- Benjamin Davidson, <u>The Analytical Hebrew and Chaldee Lexicon</u>, (London, Samuel Bagster)

- Isaac Mozeson, <u>The Word: the Dictionary that reveals the Hebrew origin of English</u> (New York. Slapsky)
- Ehud Ben-Yehuda, David Weinstein, <u>English-Hebrew Hebrew-English Dictionary</u>, (N.Y., Washington Square Press, Inc., 1961)
- Rev. Walter W. Skeat, <u>A Concise Etymological Dictionary of the English Language</u>, (N.Y., Capricorn Books, 1963)

Hebrew Thought
- Mary Ellen Chase, <u>Life and Language in the Old Testament</u> (N.Y., W. W. Norton and Company Inc., 1955)
- Thorleif Boman, <u>Hebrew Thought Compared with Greek</u> (N.Y., W.W. Norton and Company, 1960)

Hebrew Language
- <u>Gesenius' Hebrew Grammar</u>, (London, Oxford Press, 2nd English Ed. 1910)
- William R. Harper, <u>Elements of Hebrew</u>, (N.Y., Charles Scribner's Sons, 1895)
- Edward Horowitz, <u>How the Hebrew Language Grew</u> (KTAV, 1960)

Ancient Language and Origins
- John Philip Cohane <u>The Key</u> (N.Y., Crown Publishers, 1969)
- Charlton Laird <u>The Miracle of Language</u> (Greenwich Conn., Fawcett, 1953)
- Giorgio Fano, <u>The Origins and Nature of Language</u>, (Bloomington In., Indiana University Press, 1992)

Bibles

- Biblia Hebraica Stutgartensia
- The Holy Bible, New International Version (Grand Rapids, Zondervan Bible Publishers, 1973, 1978, 1984)
- The Stone Edition Tanach (Brooklyn, Mesorah Publications Ltd., 1996)
- The Holy Bible, King James Version

Notes

Notes

Ancient Hebrew Language and Alphabet

Printed in the United States
47373LVS00002B/379

9 781589 395343